Linux

The ultimate crash course to learn Linux,
system administration, network security, and
cloud computing with examples and exercises

Mark Reed

Table of Contents

Introduction

You have probably heard Linux mentioned somewhere. However, you might not have given it much thought since most people think that it is too difficult and only meant for computer gurus or enthusiasts who want to explore their machine more. However, this is far from the truth. Linux is a simple system that takes a different approach to how an operating system should work.

Let's say you own a vehicle; you don't really have to know everything about combustion engines to understand that they make the car move or know the principles of hydraulics to understand what's wrong when stepping on the brake pedal does nothing to slow down the car. Just like the combustion engine, an operating system handles the inner workings of your computer and ensures that everything runs smoothly. Sometimes things go wrong; in many cases you have a helpline number you can call when problems arise, and they get dealt with. If your car breaks down, you can call any breakdown car service to assist you. The same applies to computers.

Still, even if you get help and the problem is solved, such as with a broken-down car or crashed computer, many people don't understand the explanation given as to why the problem occurred in the first place. If they understood this information, it would help them deal with this issue if it recurred.

Having fundamental knowledge about the principles of an operating system and how it works gives you an upper hand and places you in a better position to understand and deal with problems as they arise. Also, if you know something or someone, you tend to have a better attitude and relationship with them. Just like with a car, if you hear weird noises every time you apply the brake, you know that you need to check on the brake pads and see if they need to be replaced. For computers, this is what Linux does. It gives you an all-access pass into the inner workings of your computer and other systems so you have a better understanding of your equipment. With the many advances in hardware design and performance, computers nowadays can process more data. With Linux, you can harness this computing power to the fullest.

Linux is a fantastic technology and the basis of many systems that we use today. It has grown from the hobby of one man to a worldwide sensation. With its vast applications, it pays to know more about Linux, and even you can become a pro at it.

This book is intended for anyone looking to learn more about Linux or as a reference guide for advanced users. It has examples and exercises to help you get a better understanding of the Linux system and to try things out on your own. It is structured to comprehensively teach you about Linux even if you are a beginner and provide you with the requisite skill set you require to take advantage of the versatility of this system. Having that in mind, let's take a look at what you will be learning in this book.

In chapter one, we will look at installing and setting up your operating system. You will learn about the various distributions of the Linux OS and how to select the right one for you. You will also learn about preparing your computer, installing software, setting up the system, upgrading, and more. At the close of the chapter, you will have enough knowledge to know which system to install and set up. In the second chapter, we will examine the desktop environments and dive deeper into the setup process. The third chapter is about system interaction. We will discuss how the Linux system interacts with various files, hardware, and even other system components. Chapter four takes a look at system administration and everything it entails. The fifth chapter is on security. It explains how you can secure your system since Linux is open-source, what the threats are, and how to deal with them. We will also delve into network security, and you will learn how to set up firewalls and how to protect yourself from hackers. Chapter six covers networking in Linux and all it entails. The final section is on cloud computing and how Linux has impacted this sector. At the end of every chapter, there will be some exercises you can do to help you internalize the theoretical concepts taught.

Chapter One:
Installation and Setting Up Your System

Before getting into what Linux is, you must understand what an operating system is. It is common to find users who have no clue what an operating system is or what operating system they are using. When you turn on your computer, you see a screen where you can write, draw, surf the web, play music, watch videos, and more. Ever asked yourself what makes the computer hardware, such as the mouse, screen, or keyboard, work the way it does? How does your computer processor know that you want to play a video file?

The operating system is responsible for how your computer works and acts as an interface between you and your computer. These systems are basically managers that are in charge of computer system resources. These resources include RAM, ROM, the monitor, the hard disk, or any connected devices. The operating system has management functions that determine who gets to access data from the hard disk, what appears on the screen next when you select a file, or how much memory a program gets.

There are many operating systems available, such as Windows, Mac OS, iOS, and Linux. Some of these systems are proprietary such as Windows, while others like Linux are open-source. What this means is that with open-source tools, you can examine and analyze the source code and make any modifications you want. This high level of customization sets Linux apart from other operating systems because you have complete control over what you want your computer to do.

In the beginning, Linux developers concentrated more on the networking and service aspects of the system. This made it a favorite among hobbyists but kept it from penetrating the desktop market. Many people still think that Linux is complicated because everything is done in text mode. However, the Linux community has worked hard to turn this system into one that can be used on a workstation as well as on midrange and high-end servers.

Today Linux is readily available either online or from local retailers. Users can now even purchase computers that come with a pre-installed Linux distribution. In the early days, you had to be an expert or have a solid background in computing to use Linux, but companies such as RedHat, Mandriva, and SuSE arose to provide versions of Linux that can be used by the masses. They integrated many components, such as graphic user interfaces (GUIs) developed by the Linux community to ease program and service management. With the addition of these user-friendly interfaces and MS Office-compatible programs such as word processors, Linux is quickly becoming an acceptable choice for everyday home or office use. Its application spans further than just being a workstation or a server OS. It also runs on gadgets such as phones, tablets, or even smartwatches. This makes Linux the only OS that interacts with such a wide range of hardware.

In this section, we'll take a look at how to select and install Linux onto your computer. We will also get into how to set up the system, troubleshoot, and even update or upgrade to a new Linux version.

Selecting a Linux Distribution

As mentioned above, it was pretty hard to use Linux in the beginning. Many people chose not to learn it because even though documentation on every aspect of the system existed, the explanations were too technical for newbies to understand, thus discouraging them from learning the system. This realization pushed the Linux community to make changes to the accessibility of the system and make it more appealing to more non-techy people.

This paved the way for the development of Linux distributions which did not require that you have an in-depth knowledge of Linux to use them or have the system comply with your commands. Nowadays, you can log in and start all the applications you want without having to type a single command and still have the ability to access the system core if need be. This system allows new users to get accustomed to the system instead of being forced to learn things the hard way.

So what is a Linux distribution? Linux distributions are the many operating systems created by various programmers, organizations, or companies that are individually tailored to suit their needs. They combine the Linux kernel and other software such as the GNU core utilities, graphical servers, a desktop environment, programs, and more. Each distribution has a different combination of these elements as they are built for a specific purpose to meet the needs of its intended users.

More and more Linux distributions are now being made for desktop users who are generally considered to be the least likely to know how a system works. The developers are working to create beautiful desktops or at least make them look like your former Windows or Mac workstation and compatible programs. There are a lot of sites with screenshots that can show you how your computer will look once you install Linux. Most of these distros can be downloaded for free and burned onto a CD or USB or installed in any machine you want. Here are some of the most popular Linux distributions:

- Linux Mint

- Manjaro

- Debian

- Ubuntu

- RedHat Enterprise

- Fedora

- CentOS

- Opensuse

There are many Linux distributions available, meaning that you are sure to find one that suits your needs, and you don't have to be an expert to get a suitable version. However, this also makes selecting a Linux distribution an overwhelming task. So how do you choose one?

The distro you will use will depend on how you answer the following questions: How excellent are your computer skills? Do you favor a modern or a regulation desktop interface? Are you using Linux for a server or desktop? For someone with reasonably basic computer skills, you will want to stick to the more newbie-friendly distributions such as Linux Mint, Ubuntu, etc. However, if your skillset ranges further than this average range, you can go for distros such as Fedora or Debian. If you have mastered computers and system administration, you can pick Gentoo or take on a challenge and build your own Linux distribution from scratch.

For a server-only distro, you have to choose if you need to have a desktop interface, or you want to use command lines only. Command-line only server distributions are not weighed down by graphics, but you will need to have a good understanding of the Linux command line. You can install a graphical user interface package in the server distro with the command line as well; for example, you can get Ubuntu-desktop by typing `sudo apt-get install ubuntu-desktop`. Also, while selecting a server distribution, do you want one that offers you everything you need when you download it, or do you want to adapt a desktop distro to serve your needs?

It is essential to consider your hardware when selecting a Linux distro. Since all distributions have similar basic packages based on the Linux kernel, what you should focus on is whether the distro you want will run on your hardware. For instance, LinuxPPC was made to run on Apple and other

13

PowerPCs and does not work with x86 based devices. It can run on newer Mac computers, but you cannot use it on older machines because the technology is now obsolete.

Hardware Checklist

You can install Linux on any computer; however, this also depends on the kind of Linux distribution you are installing and what you plan on using the computer for. Here are some basic requirements for any machine running a Linux distro.

1.   CPU

This is the brains of the computer, and it defines the speed at which your OS will run. Since Linux was initially designed to work on an Intel 386, it can pretty much run on any CPU. You can also run Linux on a Mac or even ARM-based machines such as Raspberry Pi. However, Linux distributions are popular on x64 (64 bit) intel or AMD PPC (G3-G5) and AMD processors, and today they are actively developed for these devices. The minimum requirements for a CPU are 2GHz Intel Pentium 4 or AMD K6 with a dual-processor. This will run the OS, but the desktop experience will be limited. If you can, get a computer with better or higher specifications.

2.   RAM (memory)

Most distros will require about 2 GB of RAM to run any graphical interfaces. However, if you want to utilize it for non-graphical based uses such as web page hosting, you can even run Linux with less than 10 MB of RAM. For better performance, the minimum RAM should 512 MB upwards.

3.   Hard Disk Drive

As with all things in Linux, it is possible to do it even in the smallest of setups. Certain distributions such as Puppy Linux can be run with a few hundred megabytes. However, for standard desktop installations, you will need about 20–40 GB of free space on your hard drive. This is enough space to let you explore the OS more. If you plan on converting your entire system to Linux, then the more space you have, the better. Newer Linux distros now support new drive technology such as RAID and SATA out the box, with enterprise-grade fiber channel disk arrays supported by Linux server distributions.

Typically, Windows occupies 100% of the space on your computer, so to install Linux, you will have to repartition your hard disk and make some room. Newer distributions have made it even easier to partition your drive by making use of the free space on your HDD. If you are resizing your drive, try to give

Linux as much space as you can. Don't forget to allocate some space for SWAP. SWAP is the area in which, if the RAM on your machine fills up, it will use this disk space instead. This is useful if you only have limited RAM, however on higher RAM specs, you probably won't need it. You can also set up your Linux OS on a separate hard drive if you have one. This way you don't mess around with system files as you are resizing partitions

4.   Video Cards or the Graphics Adaptor

Any graphics adaptor will work with Linux as long as your computer supports it. The minimum specification is having a standard graphics card capable of 1024 x 768 resolution. Ideally, a 3D accelerated graphics card with about 256 MB graphics RAM works well.

Preparing for Installation

Once you have selected the distribution you want to install, you can download the .iso files for free from their respective websites, as well as a list of recommended system requirements for the distro. Despite what many think, installing Linux is very easy, as most versions have what is called a live distribution. This means that the OS will run from whichever device, either a CD/DVD, USB, or external drive, without making changes to your hard drive.

16

This allows you to get full functionality without committing to an installation. Once you have gotten used to it, you can decide whether to install it or not by double-clicking on the install button and following the wizard prompts.

There are various ways you can install your Linux OS:

1.   Using a USB Stick

You can install your desired Linux distro onto your computer via a bootable USB stick. After downloading the OS files onto your computer, download a universal USB installer to make your USB stick bootable. Then follow the prompts to install Linux onto the USB drive. After the operating system has been installed and configured, a small window will appear to let you know that your USB stick now ready.

2.   Using a CD-ROM

Just like the USB drive, download the .iso files and burn them onto a CD, which you will then use to boot your computer in Linux.

3.   Using Virtual Machine

This is a popular method of installing Linux. The virtual installation allows you to run your Linux

OS in a machine with an existing operating system. For instance, you can have both Windows and Linux running on the same machine. Virtual machine software such as Oracle VM can install Linux distributions in the following easy steps. First, download and install a virtual box that suits your machine. Once the setup is done, download the operating system files and create a virtual machine to install the OS. Follow the prompts to set up the virtual machine where your Linux OS will reside. After you are done, you have the option to install the operating system or run it without installing it. There are additional steps in the installation process, such as setting up user accounts, which we'll examine later.

Setting up the System

During installation, you configured some basics, such as selecting your preferred language, keyboard layout, and time zone. The next step prompted you to create a user name and password and also provide other login information such as your name and the computer's name to enable the installation of the Linux distro. This is the password you need to log into your account and perform any administrative tasks. In this pop-up box, you could also choose whether to let the system log you in automatically or require your password with every login. This step is vital if you plan on sharing your computer. It acts as an added layer of protection against any user making unsolicited changes.

After installation, your computer will reboot and display its desktop environment. At this point, you must perform a hardware check after the system restarts. Most of the hardware should work right out of the box with any Linux distro that has been installed, although you may be required to download additional drivers to get everything working well. This is because some hardware, such as graphics cards, require proprietary drivers to work. There is an open-source driver that will work with the card, but to get the most out of it you will have to obtain the drivers from the manufacturer.

Command Line Interface

The Linux command line is a text interface that allows you to communicate with the computer, and it is solely based on textual input and output. A command is an instruction that is given to a computer instructing it on what to do. They are generally given by typing them in a command line and pressing enter. An all-text display mode, also known as the command-line interface, can consist of a console and a terminal window to display the command prompt. The command prompt or shell prompt is a short, automatically generated text message that appears at the beginning of the command line. It shows the user that the system is ready for the next command, data element, or other input and also helps the user to plan and execute the following operations.

On the default shell on Linux, the bash shell, the command prompt contains the username, computer name, and the name of the current directory. For example, if a user named X is working in a directory named *research* on a computer named *home*, the shell prompt would look like this: `[X@home research] $`

The terms command line, shell prompt, and command prompt are used interchangeably, especially when providing instructions on the commands being issued. For instance, an instruction might say, "Input the following at the command line," "Input the following at the shell prompt," or "Input the following at the command prompt."

There are two ways to obtain the shell prompt when using a GUI. Open the terminal window by clicking on the terminal window icon or menu item or switching from the graphical user interface to a console without closing any open programs, or press the CTRL, ALT, and F1 keys together, and the shell prompt will appear. After you are done, you can restore the GUI by pressing the ALT and F7 keys.

Updating the System

Even though Linux has become more user-friendly, its systems are still fundamentally different from Windows or Mac, and it is best to understand these systems in order to use them well. There are two ways you can update your system in Linux, either using the command line or by using the update manager. You must understand that when updating Linux, every distro handles this process differently. This is because some distros are distinctly different down to the kind of files they use for their package management. For instance, Ubuntu and Debian use .deb, Fedora and SuSE use .rpm, etc. Another difference is whether during installation the distro is installed from source code or pre-compiled .bin or .package files.

Let us take Ubuntu, for instance, as an example of how you can update your Linux system. The Ubuntu distro uses two different tools to update the system, the apt-get command-line tool and the update manager, which is a GUI tool.

1.   Using the Update Manager

The update manager is nearly a completely automatic tool, which saves you the trouble of constantly monitoring your system to see if new updates are available. If updates are available, the update manager will pop up, depending on the urgency of the update. Security updates are set to appear daily and non-security updates weekly. You can also check for updates manually by clicking on the Administration sub-menu on the System menu and select the update manager. Once you open the manager, click on the Check button to see if there are new updates available.

To update your system, check to see if the updates selected are the ones you want to install. By default, all updates are selected. Next, click on the Updates button, enter your superuser (sudo) password, and click OK. The system will automatically install the updates in the background, allowing you to continue with your work. Some updates such as kernel update require that you log out, log back in, or restart your machine. Once the updating is done, the update manager will pop up on the screen to report that your system is now up-to-date.

2.   Using the Command-line Tool Apt-Get

Ubuntu's package manager is called apt. It is a powerful tool that manages all your system packages via the command line. Using it to update your system does have one drawback: you have to check for updates continually. To use this method, open a terminal window and type *sudo apt-get upgrade*. You will be requested to input your password. Next, a list of the available upgrades will appear, and you can go over them. To accept all the updates, click on the Y key and hit enter. This will install the updates.

Chapter Summary

In this chapter, we have learned:

- What Linux is and that an OS based on the Linux kernel or shell is called a distribution or distro

- There are numerous distributions available, some of which are designed to accomplish a sole purpose like running servers or act as network switches.

- Linux can be installed on your computer system via USB stick, CD-ROM, or virtual installation

- What the Linux command line is and how to interact with the OS using it.

- How to update your Linux OS.

Exercises

Here are a few practical exercises for beginners.

Exercise 1: Select a Linux distribution and install it on your PC

Important tip: ensure that you read the information provided thoroughly to prevent causing any errors. Read every installation message carefully to make sure you install the OS successfully. Refer to the notes in this chapter if you need help.

Exercise 2: Installing Operating System packages using the apt tool

• Use the apt command-line tool to install the `clustalw` multiple alignment tool and the `clustalx` graphical user interface

• Take note of how many additional packages were required to satisfy the mandates for each tool

• Use the `clustalx` tool to align the rRNA sequences in `Align_Data/reference_sequences.txt`

• You can use the `apt-file` program to view which files have been installed by a specific package. Use this to view what was installed by the `clustalw` package

24

- Install apt-file with `apt install apt-file` (as root)

- Build the file cache with `apt-file update`

- List the files for `clustalw` with `apt-file list clustalw`

- Look at the directories the files are installed into

Exercise 3: Installing Linux in a VM

- Select a live Linux distro to install such as Ubuntu live and download its .iso image file

- Next set up a new VM and allocate some memory to it, (2GB) and on the hard disk (20GB)

- Add the ISO to the virtual DVD drive and start the step-by-step installation process until you successfully install the Linux distribution

Chapter Two:
Desktop Environment

One of Linux's most distinctive features is its capacity for customization. You can adapt any aspect of the operating system to suit your specific needs, and this gives it a leg over other operating systems such as Windows or MacOS. For example, let's assume you want to install Ubuntu, which is a safe, user-friendly choice. However, there are about eight official different flavors of Ubuntu that behave and look different, and this mostly comes down to the type of desktop environment each is using.

Before you can fully understand what a desktop environment is accurately, let us expound a bit more on operating systems. All operating systems such as Windows, Linux, or MacOS have a kernel or shell which directly controls your computer hardware and translates any commands that are given by a piece of software into something that your equipment can understand. This way, it knows what to do when executing a command. The kernel also manages your hardware resources, such as memory management, for the various software you will be using intelligently.

So, in a nutshell, the kernel is the brain or the engine of the system, and it acts as a mediator between the software and hardware. However, this is not something beginners should worry about too much, as most of the interaction with the computer system will be via a graphical user interface. This is typically what a desktop environment is.

A desktop environment combines various components such as icons, menus, toolbars, and desktop widgets to provide a common GUI. They also include a set of integrated computer applications and utilities, but most importantly, they have their own windows manager, although it can be replaced with another compatible one. A computer user is free to configure their graphical user interface as they please, and desktop environments provide a simple way to accomplish this task.

Users are also free to mix and match applications from several environments. For instance, a GNOME user can run KDE applications such as the Konqueror web browser if they prefer it over GNOME's Epiphany web browser. However, one major drawback to using this mix and match approach is that many of these applications often rely heavily on the underlying libraries of their respective desktop environments (DE). This means that to install these applications, you will have to install a large number of dependencies, which can take up a lot of disk space. To avoid this, users can stick to using one desktop environment or choose alternatives that depend on fewer external libraries.

One advantage of using DE-provided applications in their native environments is that they tend to work better. Mixing and matching can result in visual discrepancies, such as having interfaces that use different icons or widgets than those installed, or imported elements not working as they should, which can cause confusion and result in the system behaving unexpectedly.

It is important to note that every environment is distinct in its nature and purpose. Deciding which DE to use will depend on your needs. Also, before installing a desktop environment, you need to install a functional X server because most environments support it. Although others also support Wayland as an alternative to X, many of these DE are still experimental. We shall take a more in-depth look into the X window system later on, but you can also visit X.org for more information.

Types of Desktop Environments

Below are some examples of officially supported desktop environments available to Linux users.

1.   GNOME

This is a prevalent desktop environment among Linux users. It is free, open-source, simple yet powerful, and easy to use. It is so popular that other desktop environments referred to as "forks" were developed from it. These include Cinnamon, Unity, etc. It was designed to be highly customizable, thus giving Linux desktop users a pleasant computing experience. GNOME key features include a dashboard that shows an overview of all your activities, a system-wide search tool, powerful in-house applications, themes, extension support, and window snapping.

Its latest release, GNOME 3, showcases a modern, attractive user interface, and it also aims to provide better support for touch input devices. In addition, it now uses Metacity as its default window manager, and Nautilus comes as the default file manager with Google Drive integration. It supports desktop notifications using a convenient messaging system that you can turn on and off.

Some of the advantages of using this DE include its modern and touch-friendly user interface. You can also extend its functionalities by using GNOME shell extensions, and it is highly customizable. Some drawbacks include its hefty utilization of computer resources, such as the memory, compared to other alternatives because of its heavily graphical interface, and some of its extension management is unsatisfactory. Also, to customize this DE, you need a gnome-tweaking tool. Some of the major distros that use GNOME include Ubuntu GNOME, OpenSuSE, Debian, and Fedora.

2. KDE

This is another popular desktop environment — and the most highly customizable — because it is designed to give Linux users complete control over their desktop. KDE is more than a desktop environment. It is a collection of apps that include the DE. Where other environments require you to have a tweaking tool installed, for KDE it is all in the system settings. This allows you to personalize your desktop without using third-party tools, and you can even download widgets, wallpapers, and themes without using the web browser.

It offers a collection of basic applications you can use, and it is also compatible with other apps even if they were not developed using the KDE Development Platform. These built-in apps come bundled with a variety of essential features that are often absent in the alternative. KDE is an excellent choice whether you need a desktop environment that works out of the box or one that can be fully customized to suit your needs.

Some of its perks include being the most advanced, powerful, and feature-rich DE with a polished user interface. It also gives users a highly customizable and flexible experience with its wide range of applications and software compatibility. However, it does have some slightly heavy resource usage, and some components appear too complicated to use.

Its latest version, known as Plasma, is available in two variants: Plasma Desktop and Plasma Netbook. The Plasma 5 release includes features such as the Dolphin file manager and the Kwin windows manager. It has a converged shell with updated graphics stacks to enable smoother graphics performance. There are also workflow improvements made in the desktop notification area, modern launchers, and better support for high-density display (high DPI) and more minor features. Some distros that use KDE as their default include openSuSE and Kubuntu.

3.   Xfce

The Xfce desktop environment truly embodies the traditional UNIX philosophy of modularity and reusability. It has several components that provide the full functionality one can expect of a modern DE while remaining relatively light. They are packaged separately, and you can select among the available packages to create your optimal working environment.

It is lightweight and easily adaptable to old hardware. It also has a modern, visually appealing look, and it is highly customizable. It comes installed with the Xfwm file manager and Thunar file manager. The user session manager handles logins, power management, etc. and you can set the background image, icons, widgets, and more through the desktop manager. It is, however, not touch-friendly, so it is not ideal for devices that have touch input. Manjaro Linux and Xubuntu use Xfce as the default desktop environment.

4.   Cinnamon

Cinnamon was initially developed to be the default desktop environment for Linux Mint. It is a combination of several projects such as Cinnamon — a fork of the GNOME shell, Cinnamon screensaver, Cinnamon desktop, Cinnamon Menus, Cinnamon Settings Daemon, and more. Cinnamon has various customizable elements, such as panels, themes, and extensions. Since it is based on GNOME, it comes with several basic applications from GNOME. This DE also features the MDM display manager, Nemo file manager, Muffin window manager, Cinnamon session manager, Cinnamon translations, Blueberry — a Bluetooth configuration tool, and more.

Some of Cinnamon's perks include its sleek polished look, familiar interface, and customization capacity. Its small icons are not touch-friendly, thus it making it hard to use on touch devices.

Desktop Environment Implementation

A system that offers a DE, a window manager, and applications written using a widget toolkit are accountable for most of what the user sees. The window manager supports the user's interactions with the DE, while the toolkit provides a developer with a library for applications that look and behave in a similar manner. A windowing system such a X or Wayland interfaces directly with the OS and libraries and provides the needed support for graphical hardware and input devices like keyboards.

The window manager operates on top of this windowing system, and while the latter provides window management functionality, it is still seen as part of the window manager. Applications designed to work with a particular manager in mind are made using a windowing toolkit, which is provided by the OS or window manager. This toolkit allows the applications to access widgets that let the user interact with the apps.

Some factors can influence a user's choice of DE; these include:

●　　The look and feel of the desktop environment. Some users are comfortable with a certain look or feel which they are familiar with. This is especially true for newbies or users who are transitioning from Windows or Mac to Linux. They might go for DE that has similar layouts to their previous operating systems.

• Flexibility and configurability. Experienced users may opt for DEs that are more configurable or customizable so that they can tune it to work how they want. For beginners, many prefer an easy-to-use environment that they can get used to quickly.

• Personal software preferences. Each DE comes with default software applications and a default way of how things are done. A new or casual user may want a graphic-rich interface, while a more experienced user may opt for a more straightforward interface or even user command-line interface tools.

The X Window System

The X Window System is often referred to as the distributed, graphical method of working. It is an open-source, cross-platform, client-server, computer software program that provides a GUI in a distributed environment. It is distributed because you could run the display on a monitor in one location, even though the application is running on a computer somewhere else. The graphical aspect is brought in by the images and other graphics that are displayed on your screen. Despite how popular it is among UNIX users, it is not a UNIX product. It was developed in 1994 by the Massachusetts Institute of Technology (MIT) and Stanford University, and operates on a wide range of machines, even MS Windows-based versions. The X.Org Foundation is an open group that manages the development and standardization of X.

The X Window System, also known as simply X or X11, provides the basic framework for a GUI environment. At the base level, X uses the elements of the GUI on the user's screen and constructs methods for sending user interactions back to the software. Using application GUI development toolkits, an application developer can create an application interface. Because X has been designed to use a client/server model from the beginning, it is well suited for remote application use as well, letting you work from your computer directly with an application running on another computer. X is also hardware-independent, meaning you can run MS applications on a UNIX workstation. Some of its features include network transparency, customizable graphical capability, and the ability to link to different networks.

X Architecture

We already know that X was designed using client-server architecture, the X.Org server, and the X terminal. Here the applications themselves are the clients because they communicate with the server, issue requests, and also receive information from other servers. The X server, however, retains exclusive control of the display and service requests from the clients. Applications only need know how to talk to the server and not bother with the actual graphics display device. The advantages of utilizing this model are pretty clear here. At the fundamental level, an application (client) can tell the server to execute specific instructions such as "draw a circle."

This would be no different from using a graphics library to write the application; however, X goes a step further. It does not require the application to be on the same computer as the server. This is because the protocols used to communicate between the client and server can work over a network or even on any inter-process communication mechanism that provides a reliable octet-stream. The preferable way to do this is by using TCP/IP protocols. Here is an example to better illustrate how powerful the X system is: you can run a processor-intensive application on your Dell computer, run a database monitor on a Solaris server while using an email application on a small BSD mail server, and use a visualization program on another server to display all this information on your Linux workstation.

It is clear that the X server is handling the graphics display. Since it runs on the actual computer or device the user is using, it's the server's responsibility to interact with the user. This means reading the input devices and relaying this information to the client so it can react appropriately. X also has a library named Xlib that handles all low-level client-server communications. The client has to use functions contained in the library to get tasks done.

The Client/Server Relationship

X is based off a client-server architecture and is activated as a combination of the server and client programs. Here the terms "client" and "server" are used to refer to local and remote devices. Below are more client-server terminologies.

- X server – this refers to a program run on a local host that is connected to the user's display and input devices

- X client – refers to a program that runs on a remote host and processes data while communicating with the X server

- Application server – a program that also runs on a remote host that processes data and communicates with application clients

● Application client – a program run on a local host that is connected to the user's display and input devices

Modern X servers have the MIT shared memory extension and can talk with their local clients using local shared memory. This negates the need for network-transparent Xlib inter-process communication and enables the system to render larger images.

The X windowing system works like all client-server models where the X server contains several resources that it provides to the client. As stated earlier, the server and the client programs don't have to be on the same machine because X is included in the TCP/IP protocol. And since X is more of a protocol than a program, computers can still communicate even if they have different architectures. For instance, a digital OSF/I server can service a Linux and AIX client as well as either client system providing services to the OSF/I server. Similar to other network applications, a single machine can serve as a client or server.

The server interfaces between the application and the hardware, so when you input data through an input device, it is responsible for relaying this data to the application. This is referred to as an event. When a user presses a key, it causes an event that the application must react to. For example, if you click on a particular menu item, this event is relayed to the client application, which responds by requesting the server to show the pull-down menu. The server then passes this info onto the hardware, which shows the menu on a screen. A product of this separation of functionality is that one client could display info on several servers.

To start any process, an X server has to be running somewhere either on the same machine or network as the client. Some systems have a graphic login that starts automatically on booting in the desktop environment. Alternatively, the system can begin through the `startx` shell script. The command reads the `.xinitrc` and `.xserverrc` files in the home directory and treats them similarly to how the shell would manage the `.cshrc` and the `.kshrc` files. This is where applications such as the terminal window and the window manager are initiated.

Configuring the X Window System

In the early days of the X windowing system, configuring a display meant that you had to have an intensive knowledge of the display's capabilities and the ability to express data about the resolution, position, color depth, font, and more. Since the arrival of the Video Electronics Standards Association (VESA) and display data channel (DDC) protocols, which allow a display to communicate these capabilities into a graphics card and then to the computer, configuration became more automatic. Configuring your hardware devices has also become a lot easier; you plug them in and start using them.

However, as with everything in Linux, there is an underlying configuration that you can use. In fact, the X.org implementation of X gets this information from several sources, the main one being the xorg.conf file. It also includes the files from the `xorg.conf.d` directory, which is located in `/etc/X11`. You can add additional configurations from the command line, desktop environment variables, auto-detection, or restoration defaults. However, you do not have to worry too much as most distros come with a configuration tool that configures X for you, or at least presents it in a less complex way.

Also, the Xorg setting command can automatically detect devices, so this negates the need for advanced editing. You might need to edit the directory if your hardware or equipment does not show up. Be extremely careful, as making any changes in the server can cause your machine to not load or even damage your monitor. There is also the possibility of permanently damaging your computer that accompanies editing any system file.

Hardware and X

We know that the X server controls the input and output devices, and since new hardware is being developed every day, we cannot be very specific about hardware compatibility. To help, here are some generalities.

● As a rule of thumb, if the device uses a commonplace protocol such as PS/1 or PS/2, it should be well supported. However, if it is still new tech, the chances are that it might not be supported yet.

● For monitors – Linux doesn't have to be compatible with any specific monitor because this is the job of the video card. As long as your graphics card works with the monitor, then it should work.

● For video cards – the X server is determined by the chipset, and naturally, a lot of them are supported. However, revisions and newer cards might not be supported yet. Newer cards are now coming with better support and optimization, and some even have advanced features such as multi-headed displays, 3D, TV-out, DRI, and more. You have to research well to find out if the card is supported. A full list of supported cards can be found online.

41

Also note that open-source drivers are developed incrementally, such that a card may work well for basic display function, but specialized features come later on in the development cycle. However, proprietary driver development differs.

● Keyboards – any keyboard should work.

● Mice and other pointing devices – most of these devices should be supported, including PS/2, bus, serial, USB, optical, and infra-red devices. Multi-button and wheeled mice are supported via the IMPS/2 or other specific protocols. However, they may need extra configuration for some applications.

You can check the hardware compatibility list on your distro's website to see what works with your release.

X Resources

Virtually all X clients are customizable. You can set how a client looks, its size, placement, background and border color or pattern, whether or not the window has a scroll bar, and more. Some applications even let users redefine the keystrokes or pointer actions used to control the program. Most traditional UNIX programs relied on command-line options to enable users to alter how they worked. Although X applications support command-line options, this does not apply to all their features. There would be too many customizable features in a program to set them all via the command line. X has an alternative to customizing an application through the command line. The X server can store several configuration values for applications, so they are readily available when needed. If the application supports it, these defaults will be used whenever the program runs. These are known as resources, and they define a user's preference on a per-application basis for colors, screen placement, and other attributes. This makes application customization even easier.

Program components are named hierarchically, with each element identified by a class and instance name. The topmost level shows the class and instance name of the app itself. The class name of an application is often the same as the program name; however, the first letter is capitalized, such as Emacs. For programs beginning with X, the second letter is also capitalized, such as XTerm. Each definition specifies an instance with the corresponding resources and values. Under this, in the hierarchy, are the many attributes that comprise the definable aspects of an application.

These resource variables can be Boolean such as `scrollBar: False` or have a numeric or string value such as `borderwidth: 4` or `foreground: green`. In applications written using the X toolkit or other object-oriented systems, resources can be linked with separate elements or widgets in a program. There is a syntax that allows for independent control over a class of elements and a singular instance of the element. For example, for a hypothetical program called *xclient:*

xclient*Buttons.foreground: yellow

xclient*help.foreground: green

The first resource specification changes the foreground color of all buttons (in the Buttons class) in the application to yellow. The second one changes the foreground color of the help button (an instance of the Buttons class) to green.

Resource values can be set as program defaults in several ways, such as including resource files in your home directory or through the X resource database (xrdb) program. Xrdb stores resources directly in the server, making them available to all clients regardless of the machine the client is running on. Placing resources in files lets you customize multiple resources at once without the restrictions encountered when using the command line. Other than having a primary resource file (named .Xdefaults or .Xresources) in your home directory that sets application defaults, you can create system-wide resource files to set program defaults. Additionally, you can create resource files to set resources for the local workstation, networked machines, or for one or more specialized machines such as servers

The resource manager sets routines that automatically read and process resource files in a certain order. The arrangement for resource specifications and the rules of precedence by which the resource manager processes them are meant to give you the most flexibility in setting resources with the minimum amount of text input. You can specify a resource that affects a single feature of a single application such as the green help button in the earlier example or define a resource variable that controls a function of multiple elements within many programs with a single line. Take note that command-line options often take precedence over other resource settings. So you can set up the files to control how the application will work normally and use the command line to specify the changes you require for an instance of the application.

Resource Naming Order

The basic syntax of a resource file is quite simple. Each client recognizes specific resource variables that can be assigned values that are documented in its reference page. Most clients are designed to utilize the X toolkit, which provides a standard set of elements or widgets like menus, dialog boxes, command buttons, etc. The naming syntax of certain resources parallels the element's hierarchy that is built into X toolkit programs. In a resource definition file, the most basic line you can have comprises the client name followed by an asterisk or a period and the name of the variable. A colon and space separate the client and variable names from the actual value of the resource variable.

For instance: `xterm*scrollBar: True`

If the client's name is absent, the variable will apply to all instances of the client. If it is specified as a global variable and a client-specific variable, the latter takes precedence for that client. However, you should note that if the client's name is omitted, the line should begin with an asterisk.

For example: `*scrollTtyOutput: False`

`*scrollKey: True`

Also, take care not to omit the colon at the end of the resource specification because the resource manager provides no error messages. If there is an error in the specification, such as a syntax error or a misspelling, it is ignored, and the value you set will not take effect. You can use the exclamation mark (!) at the beginning of the line to include a comment in the file or comment on one of the specifications. If the last character is a backslash (\), the definition is assumed to continue on the next line.

For example: `xterm*VT100.translations:`
`#override \`

`<Key>BackSpace: string(0x7F) \n\`

`<Key>Insert: string(0x1b)`
`string("[2~")\n\`

`<Key>Delete: string(0x1b)`
`string("[3~")\n\`

`<Key>Home: string(0x1b)`
`string("[1~")\n\`

`<Key>End: string(0x1b)`
`string("[4~")\n\`

`<Key>Page_Up: string(0x1b)`
`string("[5~")\n\`

`<Key>Page_Down: string(0x1b)`
`string("[6~")\n\`

```
<KeyPress>Prior : scroll-
back(1,page)\n\

<KeyPress>Next : scroll-forw(1,page)
```

Toolkit Client Resource Syntax

As stated earlier, X toolkit apps are made of widgets, and there can be a widget inside a widget; for instance, a drop-down menu in a dialog box. The syntax of resource specifications for these toolkit applications matches the levels of the widget hierarchy. You should think of a resource specification having the following format:

```
object.subobject[.subobject.   .
.].attribute: value
```

Where the object refers to the client program or a specific instance of it. The subobjects refer to the levels of widget hierarchy, the attribute is a feature of the last subobject, and the value is the actual setting of the resource. The value of a resource is clear from the resource name or the description of the variable in the reference pages. For instance, resources such as *background* take color specifications, *geometry* takes a geometry string, *font* takes a font name, etc. Logical values like those taken by *scrollBar* can be specified as either *yes* or *no, on* or *off*, or *True* or *False*

Tight and Loose Bindings

How components of a resource specification are linked is referred to as binding, and it can be done in two ways. The first is by a tight binding, which is indicated by a dot (.), or secondly by a loose binding, shown by an asterisk (*). A tight binding means that the elements on either side must be next to each other in the hierarchy. A loose binding, on the other hand — signaled by an asterisk, which is a wild character — shows that there are several levels between the two elements. You have to be very familiar with widget hierarchy to specify tight bindings, and it is not uncommon for them to be used incorrectly.

Take, for instance, this resource specification request.

```
xterm.scrollBar: True
```

This specification ignores the widget hierarchy of *xterm*, where the VT102 window, Tektronix window, and menu are all widgets. Here is the correct syntax:

```
xterm.vt100.scrollBar: True
```

A simpler alternative is to use the asterisk instead of deciphering the widget hierarchy.

```
xterm*scrollBar: True
```

49

If the program supports multiple widget levels, you can use a mix of asterisks and periods. However, using an asterisk is still recommended because it allows developers the freedom to add or remove levels in the hierarchy as they produce new releases of a program.

Classes and Instances

Every resource specification component is associated with a class, and different widget attributes can belong to the same class too. Let's say, for instance, in *xterm*, the text (*Foreground*), text cursor, and pointer color are all defined as instances of the *Foreground* class. You can, therefore, set the value of all three individuals or via a single command, as shown below:

```
xterm*foreground: limegreen

xterm*cursorColor: limegreen

xterm*pointerColor: limegreen
```

or

```
xterm*Foreground: limegreen
```

Capitalizing the first initial differentiates class and instance names. Class will always begin with an uppercase letter and instances in a lowercase one.

However, if the instance name is a compound word such as `pointer-Color`, the latter is capitalized.

The effect of class and instance naming cannot be felt in applications such as `xterm` because they have a simple widget hierarchy. In other complex applications made with the X Toolkit, this naming allows you to do more customization. Just remember that the instance name specification always overrides the class name for that instance. Class names, therefore, allow for default values to be set for all instances of a particular element. It can also be used with loose binding to specify a resource for all clients. Instance names specify the exception to the class names specifications.

Precedence Rules for Resource Specification

Resource specifications can conflict even on a singular resource file such as `.Xresources`. For instance, do you recall this example from earlier?

```
xclient*Buttons.foreground:
yellow
```

```
xclient*help.foreground: green
```

The first specification makes the foreground color for all buttons in the Buttons class yellow. The second one overrides the first specification in a single instance where it makes the foreground color of the Help button green. In such a case where specifications clash, several rules assist the resource manager in deciding which specification takes effect. These include:

- Instance names take precedence over class names

- Tight binding takes precedence over loose bindings

From the two rules, it is clear that the more specific a resource definition is, the higher it ranks and thus takes precedence. However, if you want to set things up very carefully in your system, you should know how programs interpret resource specifications. For every resource variable, a program has both a complete, fully-specified, tightly bound instance and class name. In analyzing ambiguous specifications, the program compares them against the full instance and class name. If there is a match, it is accepted. However, if more than one part in either name matches, the following rules in addition to those mentioned earlier apply.

- The hierarchy levels specified by the user must match the program's expectations or be ignored. If, for instance the program expects:

```
xterm.vt100.scrollBar:        value
instance name

XTerm.VT100.ScrollBar:        value
class name
```

The specification *xterm.scrollBar: True* won't work because the tight binding is incorrect. The elements in the xterm and scrollBar hierarchies are not adjacent. It would work if it was a loose binding.

• A class or instance name that is explicitly mentioned takes priority over one that is omitted. For instance, *xterm*scrollBar* is more specific than **scrollBar*

• Elements on the left carry more weight over those on the right, just as in the above example.

Chapter Summary

In this chapter, we looked at what a desktop environment is, the different types of DE, and their implementation. We also took a more in-depth look at the X windows system, its makeup, and configuration. It is important to note that desktop environments are preferred because they make configuring your system a lot easier compared to using the command line.

We also learned that X is a client-server, multi-user system, not just a graphical user interface. It is not integrated into the OS but instead operates on top of it like other servers. It is also an open standard that runs on many platforms. What you see on the screen is a combination of many components working together: OS, X, Window manager, and a DE if you have installed one. They are plug and play elements that let you interchange what you want without interfering with the rest. Since they all have their configurations, this makes the system very robust and flexible, although it makes it quite complex.

Exercises

1.   Explore the menus in your desktop environment. What happened?

2.   Customize your terminal window. Were you successful?

3.   Configure your window manager and try out different workspaces (virtual screens).

4.   Apply a different theme. Were you successful?

5.   Switch to a different window manager. What happened?

6.   Log out and pick a different session type, like Cinnamon, if you were using Gnome earlier. Repeat the previous steps.

Chapter Three:
The Shell and Its Utilities

By now, as a Linux user, you are already aware of the basic makeup of a Linux system. It is comprised of a kernel, Shell, commands and utility programs, files, and directories. The kernel is the core of the operating system. It interfaces with the computer hardware and other core functions such as memory management, file management, and task scheduling. Shell is a utility program that handles your requests. When a user enters a command into the terminal, Shell deciphers the commands and initiates the program you want to helps generate the result you wanted. It uses a standard order for all its commands. There are several shells available for Linux distros such as C shell, Bash, Korn Shell, and many more.

The commands and service programs comprise the commands mentioned above and other utility programs that the user uses. These include mkdir, sudo, cp, cal, and so on. There are over two hundred and fifty standardized commands plus numerous troves of those supplied through 3rd party software. All of the data in a Linux system is arranged in files. These files are then arranged into directories. This organization structure further arranges the directories into a tree-inspired structure known as the file system.

In this and subsequent chapters, we will take a more in-depth look into these various components and see how they work on a Linux system, as well as how you can utilize them. The first one you will tackle is Shell and its utilities.

Shell

As a refresher, the Shell is, in essence, an interface between the OS and the user. It is a command-line interpreter through which you can issue various instructions to the system. The Shell interprets these instructions, and it tells the system what actions to take. Therefore, the command prompt is where you input these instructions or commands. Before GUIs were developed, the only way to input commands was via the Shell prompt. All these shells have similar input attributes. You have to issue commands to get the device to carry out any task.

Some commands do not require any input to work, such as the date command; however, others require an argument or option to work. Anything included in the command line after the command is an argument. An option affects this behavior, whereas an argument is acted upon as is by the command. It is important to note that some arguments are optional, and other options are needed. For instance, you don't always require an argument for the date command, whereas the tar command requires an option.

The basic Shell of all Unix systems is the Bourne shell, simply denoted as (sh). Other shells such as bash, csh, ksh, and more have evolved from this. Every Shell has a certain order in which the internal functions such as the variables, redirection of input and output devices, etc. are executed. There are many advantages to learning how to use the Shell and its functions. Let's take a look at some of its components below.

Environment Variables

The shell environment consists of everything it will need as it runs. These components are referred to as environment variables and include the search path, the user's logname, and the type of terminal you are using. When a user logs in, many of these variables are already set by a shell mechanism.

An environmental variable is a variable with a name and value. This value can be anything from the default editor, system locale settings, to even directories. PATH is an example of such a variable. New Linux users find these settings' management somewhat hard to handle. Environmental variables, however, offer a simpler way to share configuration settings among many programs and processes. The following are some important variables you should know and how they are set and accessed.

1.　　DISPLAY – has the identifier for the default display that X11 applications use

2.　　HOME – shows the home directory of the current user, and it is the default argument for the built-in cd command

3.　　IFS – shows the Internal Field Separator used by the parser for word splitting after expansion

4.　　LD_LIBRARY_PATH – a Linux system containing a dynamic linker has a colon-separated directory list that the dynamic linker should look in for shared objects when constructing a process image after exec, before looking in other directories

5.　　PATH – shows the search path for commands

6.　　PWD – shows the current working directory as set by the cd command

7.　　RANDOM – produces an arbitrary integer within 0 and 32,767 every time it is referenced

8.　　SHLVL – increases by one every time a bash instance is initialized; it is ideal for monitoring if the built-in exit command ends the current session

9.   TERM – indicates the display type

10.   TZ – indicates the Time zone such as CAT, GMT, etc

11.   UID – expands to the numeric user ID of the current user, initialized at the shell startup

With that in mind, let us dive into the PATH environmental variable.

Paths

PATH is an environmental variable used in Linux that instructs the Shell in which directories to look for ready-to-run files as a response to user issued commands. It enhances the ease and safety of Unix-like operating systems and is thus considered quite valuable.

If, for instance, you know that there is a particular application in your system, but when you try to initialize it, the system responds with a "file not found" message. You might attribute this to you not remembering the right name or spelling. But in fact, the reason behind it is because the application was not in the search path. A user's search path is a predetermined directory set where the system searches for the application when you typed in the command line or which was initiated by another command. The search path saves the system a lot of time because it does not have to look through all the directories for what you want. By searching in specific areas, you can get faster results. The downside, however, comes when the program is not in any of the specified directories. To instruct the Shell where to look for your file, you must issue explicit commands that require you to specify either the path to the file relative to where you are or the full command path.

PATH, which is denoted in upper case letters, should not be confused with path, which is a file's or directory location in a file system. A *relative path* is a location relative to the directory which the user is currently working in. An *absolute path*, also known as a *full path*, is a location relative to the root directory. The root directory is the directory at the topmost level of the file system, and it contains all other directories and files.

A user's PATH is therefore comprised of a series of colon-separated absolute paths that are kept in plain text files. Every time a user types in commands at the command line (CL) that isn't built into the Shell or doesn't include its absolute path and hits *Enter*, the Shell looks through the directories that make up the user's search path until it finds an executable file with that name. By concentrating most executable files in a few directories and using PATH to find them, it removes the need for users to recall which directories they are in and type their absolute paths. This means that any application can be run by just typing its name, such as `ls` instead of `/bin/ls`. This execution happens regardless of whether the user is currently working on the file system. It also reduces the chance of causing damage to the data or the system by accidentally running a script named similarly to a standard command.

By running the `env` command, a user can see a list of all the current environmental variables, their values for the current user, and all the directories in the PATH variable. This command can be run without any options or arguments. Since this can be quite a bit of information, you can change the command so that it only shows the PATH variable and its value. You can do this by using a pipe that is represented by a vertical character to switch the `env` output to the `grep` filter while using PATH as an argument to `grep`, i.e., `evn|grep PATH`.

You can also use the echo command to view PATH, i.e., `echo $PATH`

Echo duplicates whatever follows it on the command line. The $ sign before PATH instructs echo to repeat the value of the PATH variable instead of the name.

Every user can have a different PATH variable. When an OS is installed, the default PATH variable, known as the root account, is created. Another default is also established that will be used as a template for other normal user accounts as they are added. The root PATH variable has more directories than the user PATH variable. This is because it contains directories such as `/sbin` and `/usr/sbin`, which contain applications used by a particular user.

PATH variables can be altered easily. You can modify them for a particular login session or alter them permanently. You can include a directory into a user's PATH variable and thus into the search path by using PATH=`"directory:$PATH"` command. For example, you can add `/usr/sbin` to the PATH variable. The command will look like this:

```
PATH="/usr/sbin:$PATH"
```

You can also use the export command to add a directory, i.e., export PATH=`$PATH:/usr/sbin`

A user's PATH variable can be made permanent by including it in the user's `.bash_profile` file. The `.bash_profile` file is a hidden file in each user's home directory that explains any particular environmental variable and startup applications for that specific user. It is important to note that a colon with no spaces should precede each absolute path. For example, PATH=$PATH:$HOME/bin:/usr/test

You might want to run an application or script that has been installed in another user's home directory or a different location other than the default search path. You can run this application or script by typing in its absolute path or preceding its command name with a dot slash, which is a period followed by a forward slash and no spaces. The dot is used to show the current directory, and the slash is a directory separator and to distinguish file and directory names.

Permissions and Access Modes

In Linux, you have to have the right permission to gain access to a file. This is important because it allows you to locate, edit, and execute commands. For instance, if you want to read a file, you must have read permission to write or edit a file, write permission, execute or run a file, or execute permission. These authorizations or access modes are set using the chmod command or during file creation. You can view a file's permissions via the l or ls -l commands

64

In Linux, file permissions are essential because they provide a secure method for file storage. Every Unix file has the following attributes: owner, group, and other or world permissions. Owner permissions define what the owner of the file can do. The group permissions show what actions can be taken by a user who is a member of the group that owns the file. Lastly, the other permissions show what actions other users can perform on a file.

As stated before, a file's permissions can be viewed through the `ls -l` command. To better comprehend what these permissions entail, let's take a look at the following example.

```
$ls -l /home/fiona

-rwxrw-r--   1 fiona   users 1024
Jan 2 00:20 myfile

drwxr-xr--   1 fiona   users 1024
Jan 2 00:20 mydir

$
```

There are ten characters at the beginning of each line, and they can either be dashes or letters. Let's break down each position accordingly.

The first place shows the file type. It can be a d for directory, r for a regular file, c for a character device, etc. The other nine places are divided into groups of three, and each group has three places to indicate the permissions granted to that group. The order for these permissions is r for read, w for write, and x for execute. The first group of three positions shows the owner's permissions, the second one shows the group permissions, and the last one shows the permissions for everyone else. If certain permissions are not granted, there will be a dash (-) in its place.

As per our above example:

d – this indicates the file type, which in this case is a directory file

rwx – this shows that the owner has all three permissions to read, write, and execute

r-x – this shows that the group can only read and execute the file

r-- - this indicates that all the other users can only read this file

For directories, if you don't have read permissions, you cannot view a directory's contents. If you lack write permissions, you cannot write to this directory. This means that you can't create a new file in that directory, either. Execute permissions mean you can search the directory and list its contents; for example, if you don't set the execution permissions, you can view directory files. Still, you cannot execute them or change into that directory. Also, if you have execute permissions but no read permissions, a user can execute files and change directories but not view the files.

Write permissions affect directories differently too because a user must have these authorizations to create a new file or remove an existing one. Even without the write permissions for the specific file, if you have directory write permissions, you can erase the files.

Modifying Owners and Groups

As you make an account in Linux, the system assigns you both an owner and group ID. These IDs influence the kind of permissions you are granted as a user. Two commands can alter the owner and group of a file. These are chown and chgrp. The first command, chown, means change owner, and it is utilized to change a file's ownership. The chgrp one stands for change group, and it changes the group of a file.

This is the basic syntax of using chown: $ chown user filelist

The value of the user can be the username or user id. Thus the above command will look something like this:

```
$ chown fiona test

$
```

This changes the file ownership to the user named Fiona. It is important to note that superusers or root users have the unrestricted ability to change file ownership, while normal users can only do so for files they own.

The syntax for chgrp is $ chgrp group filelist

Just like the previous command, the value can either be the group name or group id. The chgrp command for the above example would then be:

```
$ chgrp minor test

$
```

This changes the group of that file to minor group.

Set User ID and Set Group ID

As a command executes, it can do so with special privileges to fulfill its task. For instance, when you use the `passwd` command to alter your password, the new password is stored in the /etc/shadow file. As a regular user, you lack read and write permissions to these files because of security reasons. However, to change your password, you need these permissions. This means that the `passwd` command has to grant you this authorization to write in the /etc/shadow file. This additional permission is given to such programs through mechanisms known as Set User ID (SUID) and Set Group ID (SGID).

When a program is SUID or SGID enabled, you get the permissions of the owner and group, respectively. If they are not set, the programs use the permissions granted to the user who started them. These programs are indicated by the letter "s" if the permission is available. The "s" will appear in the slot where the owners' execute command is. Let us look at the following example:

```
$ ls -l /usr/bin/passwd

-rwsr-xr-x  1   root   bin
69531 May 7 15:49  /usr/bin/passwd*

$
```

As you can see, the SUID bit is set, and the command is a root command. An upper case "S" in place of the lowercase one would show that it is not set.

Pipes and Redirection

The | character — or as it is more commonly referred to, the pipe symbol — is quite prevalent in commands. Pipe lets you pass the output of one command through the input of another. For instance, let's say you want to make a long listing, such as the /bin directory. By inputting ls -l and hitting enter, the list appears, but the names pass by too fast to read. The entries you get to see are the last ones. If you instead input ls -l | more, the search results of the list command will be piped through more. This enables you to go through the results one batch at a time. Here the standard output of the ls command points to the pipe and becomes the standard input of the more command since it is also altered to point to the pipe.

The pipe symbol simply tells the Shell to use the files indicated instead of the standard input and output files. Every Linux system has the concepts of standard input, output, and error. Standard input is taken when a user logs in and uses the command line. Both standard output and error are sent to your screen. That is, your system expects to receive input from a keyboard or mouse and display the results or error messages on the screen.

As your system initiates, it opens these three files first. If a user, for instance, runs a command such as `find`, it gets its input from a file and shows the result on the screen. Even though it looks like the standard input is coming from the file, it's not. It is instead still coming from the keyboard. That is why, even for large files, you still use the keys to go through the results.

Filters

When an application gets input from another program or file, acts on the input, and displays the results on standard output, it is referred to as a filter. Let's look at a few of these filter commands.

The `grep` Command

This command searches a file or files for lines that exhibit a specified pattern. Here is the syntax: `$grep pattern file(s)`. The term *grep* is derived from *g/re/p*, which stands for "globally search for a regular expression and print all lines containing it." A regular expression consists of plain text and/or specialized characters used to match the patterns. The most basic use of `grep` is in searching for patterns containing single words. It can be added in a pipe so that only the input files with a certain string are output. If it doesn't have a file name to read, `grep`

71

reads its standard input. This is also how all filter programs work.

You can also use several options with grep:

- -v – shows all lines that don't match the pattern

- -n – shows the matched line and its number

- -l – (letter "l") only shows file manes with matching lines

- -c – shows the matching lines count

- -i – matches either upper or lowercase

The sort Command

This command organizes text lines alphabetically or numerically. For instance:

- $sort cars

- Alpha Romeo

- Chevy

- Ford

- Isuzu

- Mercedes

- $

However, there are several options for controlling this sorting. They include:

- -n – sorts the lines numerically and ignores blanks and tabs

- -r – reverses the sort order

- -f – sorts both upper and lowercase lines together

- +x – ignores the first x fields when sorting

You can link several commands into a pipe such as `ls -l | grep pattern file | sort +4n`

Chapter Summary

In this chapter, we looked at several things.

- The Linux Shell and what we already knew, such as its various components, and we got deeper into these elements.

- Environmental variables contain everything a shell needs to operate. An example of an environmental variable is PATH.

- We also looked at search path, absolute, and relative path too.

- The three access modes in a Linux system: read, write, and execute. These modes are also permissions as to what a user is allowed to do to a file or directory.

- There are also various commands attributed to all the actions discussed in this chapter and some examples of them in use.

Exercises

Exercise 1

a)   Run `echo $SHELL` to find out what Shell you are using.

b)   What `init` files does your shell use, and when are they used?

c)   Try out these commands and take note of the differences

- `ls`

- `ls -l`

- `ls *`

- `ls -ld*`

d)   List the contents of directories containing a *4* in their name.

Exercise 2:

a)   Use the `echo` command to display what is in your current PATH (remember it needs to be named `$PATH` when using it). Which of the directories are being searched as the command executes?

b)   Enter the following commands and observe what happens.

- `cd blah`

- `cd ..` remember to mind the space between "cd" and ".."!

- `pwd`

c)   Detail the directory contents with the `ls` command. What do you see, and what do you think these could be? Use the `pwd` command to check.

d)   Type in the `cd` command and repeat the step twice as you observe what's happening.

e)   Try `cd root` and observe what happens. Check to see which directories you have access to?

f)   Repeat the `cd` command input step, is there another way you can get to your directory?

g)   Read `man intro, man ls, and info passwd`

h)   Enter the pertinent `pwd` command.

i)   Try `man` or `info` on `cd`. Which one showed more information about `cd`?

Chapter Four:
System Administration

System administration encompasses a lot of areas, and thus it becomes quite hard to clearly define what it is precisely because all aspects of a computer fall under system administration. This includes software, hardware, networking, and even programming, to mention a few.

System administration allows a user to get a better understanding of the system and thus utilize it better, from starting the system, creating and managing accounts, installing software, configuring hardware, device management, automating the system, backing it up, etc. You can see that a system administrator wears a lot of hats. You are your system's administrator, and these responsibilities fall on you.

In this chapter, we'll examine some of those system administration tasks. We will not dive deep into the nitty-gritty, but we will cover the basics — i.e., the functional areas of system administration — so that you can use the programs and utilities at your disposal.

System Start-Up and Shut Down

Starting up a Linux system is quite simple, and it involves pressing the power button and watching your system boot. Almost all users and many system administrators have no idea of what is happening as the system boots. From switching the power on to getting to the login prompt, a lot of things must take place. Knowing what is happening in the boot process can be quite useful because you can easily tell what went wrong if a system does not start how it should. Starting up your system can be as easy as turning it on and letting it boot. However, you can alter this behavior by changing the boot process. We will not get too deep into the boot process, but here are some important things to keep in mind when shutting your system down.

Linux is unlike the other operating systems, and even with the many efforts to make it look superficially like these other operating systems, they still differ, especially when shutting the system down. In other systems, you are always aware of what's going on, and you have complete control over everything. You can decide to turn the computer off once you feel you are done. However, since Linux is a multi-user system, there are other users working or using its resources, so simply switching off the machine is not advised. Other than annoying other users, you could damage your system depending on what was running when you switched off.

On a multi-user system, there are many things that are going on without the user's awareness. For instance, the system could still have data in the buffer waiting for a chance to write it on the hard drive. If you switch off the power, this data will be lost, and the data left on the drive will be inconsistent. To prevent this, you need to shut your system down properly. What a proper shut down consists of will depend on the conditions. Linux nonetheless does have tools to help with the shutdown; switching off the power is not considered a proper shutdown.

User Account Management

When many people use a device such as a workstation, it's vital to differentiate between the users. This, for instance, helps keep their personal files private, whether it is used by many users simultaneously or only by one user at a time, such as in microcomputers. Every user is assigned a unique identifier known as a username that they use to log in.

In Unix-like systems such as Linux, there are three types of user accounts: the root, system, and user accounts. The root account, also called the super user, is automatically created when you install your Linux OS and has complete, unrestricted control over the system. In other words, it has administrative privileges for all the operating system services. A root account can run any commands, and this account is often referred to as the system administrator account. System accounts are required for the running of system-specific elements such as mail or the sshd accounts. These accounts are required for particular functions, and any modifications could affect the system badly. For instance, services such as games, mail, and printing have individual system accounts that allow them to interact with your computer. Finally, user accounts give users or groups of them interactive access to the system. These accounts have the necessary privileges to undertake standard tasks in a Linux system, such as run programs, store data in files and databases, etc. These accounts, however, do not have admin privileges, so they cannot, for example, mistakenly delete core operating system configuration files. General users are usually assigned these accounts.

Unix also supports the group account concept, where several accounts are logically grouped, making them part of the group account. This group account plays an important role in file permissions and process management. Users can be members of multiple groups. For instance, in the Red Hat Enterprise distro, when a user is added, a private user group is created.

This means that a user group named after the user has been created and the new user is the only member.

Creating an Account

The Linux system views users as numerals, and each one is assigned a unique identifying integer known as the user ID or UID. This is because, for a computer, numbers are easier and faster to process compared to textual names. There is a database outside the kernel that gives the textual name, the username, to every user ID. Every UID is assigned at least one group, with one designated as their login group.

All groups have a group ID or GID, which helps identify the user's login group. These two sets of identification help keep track of the user and define what files they can access. Applications and commands that engage with users report user data by logname or group name. However, the OS uses the UID and GID for most identification requirements. These are the primary administrative files:

- etc/passwd – stores the user account and password data; this file contains the most information about accounts on the system

- `/etc/shadow` – contains the encrypted password of the corresponding account; note that not all the systems support this file

- `/etc/group` – this file has the group's data for every account

- `/etc/gshadow` – this file has secure group account data

As stated above, the `/etc/passwd` and `/etc/group` files define both the user and group accounts, respectively, and everyone has access to them. To create a user, information about the user needs to be added to the user database and make a home directory for them, `/home/<username>`, which is also their default directory once they log into the system. It is important to note that the parent directory might differ. You might need to teach the user about a few things and set up the environment for them. There are several applications for creating user accounts available with most distributions. However, you can also use the command line to create them with the `adduser` and `useradd` commands. Let's see how to go about it.

The basic syntax for creating a new account is
`useradd [options] username`. When
expanded it looks something like this: `useradd -d
homedir -g groupname -m -s shell -u
userid account name`

- `-d homedir` – defines the home directory for the account

- `-g groupname` – defines the group account for the account

- `-m` – creates the home directory if it is non-existent

- `-s shell` – defines the default shell to use for this account

- `-u userid` – this is where you define a user id for the account

- `account name` - this is where you input your preferred account name to be created

To use this command, you must have sudo
access or be logged into a root account. The
`useradd` command makes a new user account using
the options detailed on the command line plus the
defaults in the `/etc/default/useradd` file.

These values are different in each distro; thus, running the useradd command might display varying results on each distro. The command also reads the `/etc/login.defs` file because it contains the shadow password suite configuration. These include user ID ranges used in creating accounts, password expiration policies, etc.

Type in `$ sudo useradd username` and hit enter. The command will read the default file and create an entry in the `/etc/passwd`, `/etc/shadow`, `/etc/group` and `/etc/gshadow` files. So for example, to create a new (ordinary) user account for Fiona, type in `$ sudo useradd fiona`, or `$ useradd -d /home/fiona -g minor -s /bin/ksh fiona`

Don't forget to create the minor group before issuing this command.

Changing Passwords

To log in using your new account, a password must be set using the passwd command. Here is the syntax: `$ sudo passwd username`

After running this command, you will be requested to input the password and confirm it. Ensure that you set a strong password to safeguard your account. Here is the basic syntax and an example.

```
Changing password for user username

New password:

Retype new password:

passwd: all authentication tokens
updated successfully
```

Here's the example

```
$ passwd Fiona

Changing password for user fiona

New password:

Retype new password:

passwd: all authentication tokens
updated successfully
```

Modifying Accounts

You can make changes to an existing account from the command prompt via the usermod command. It employs the same argument as the useradd and the -l commands which allow you to alter your account name. To change the account name fiona to fiona23, and alter the home directory too, you will type in: $ usermod -d /home/fiona23 -m -l fiona fiona23

Removing Accounts

You can also delete a dormant, unused, or existing account using the userdel command. Please note that this is a dangerous command and should be used cautiously. It uses only one argument or option, .r, to remove the account's mail file and home directory.

For example: $ usermod -r fiona23

If you want to retain the home directories for backup, you can omit the -r option.

Group Accounts

All the existing groups in your system are located in the /etc/groups file. However, as defaults, they are system account specific, and they are not recommended for use with ordinary accounts. To create a new group, you will use the groupadd command in the following syntax: groupadd [-g gid [-o]] [-r] [-f] group name

• -g GID – represents the numerical value of the group's ID

- -o – the option permits the user to add a group with a non-unique GID

- -r – the flag instructs the groupadd command to add a system account

- -f – this option causes an exit with success prompt if the defined group already exists. With -g, if the defined GID already exists, other (unique) GID is selected.

- groupname – this is the actual group name to be created

To modify a group, utilize the groupmod command in the following syntax: $ groupmod -n new_modified_group_name old_group_name

For example: $ groupmod -n minor minor¬_2

To delete a group, you require the groupdel command and the group's name, i.e., $ groupdel group_name. This will only remove the group and not the files.

Process Management

A process is an executable application that's operating in its own location. It is distinct from a job or command as they can comprise of several processes working together to achieve a singular task. A singular process executes simple commands such as ls. A command containing pipe symbols, for instance, is a compound command and requires the execution of several processes. By controlling the processes, you can manage the CPU resources on Unix based systems.

Don't forget that Linux is a multi-user system, so you can have several users running multiple commands simultaneously on the same system. This can present quite a challenge, and measures have to be taken for the CPU to manage all these processes while retaining functionality so users can switch between and also retrieve interrupted processes. There are cases where processes continue running even after the user who initiated them logs out.

To better understand how this works, let's examine the process structure.

Process Types

Several kinds of processes exist; here, we will look at interactive, daemons, and automatic batch processes.

Interactive Processes

These are started and controlled through a terminal session. This means a user has to be connected to the system to initiate them since they are not automatically started as part of the system functions. They can either run in the foreground or background. Processes running in the foreground remain attached to the terminal because it communicates directly with the terminal. For instance, a command that has been run and is awaiting output means it is a foreground process. While a foreground process operates, only it can get input from the terminal.

This means that if you run a command on a large file, you will not be able to run another one until the command ends, or you kill it with CTRL-C. Alternatively, you can run it as a background process. This way, the user can still use the terminal as the other program runs. This way, the system does not remain idle or generate error messages.

The shell has a feature known as job control that eases the handling of several processes. This feature switches processes from the fore to the background and vice versa. You can also start applications in the background. Running a process in the background is only useful if it does not need user input and its execution might take a while. A background process can be resumed and executed unlinked to the terminal that began it. Here are some of the ways the job control feature works in most shells.

- `regular_command` – runs a command in the foreground

- `&` - adding this to a regular command tells the shell to run the command in the background. (e.g. $ `long_cmd &`)

- `jobs` - shows a list of background processes

- Ctrl+Z – suspends, meaning it temporarily stops — but does not quit — a process running in the foreground

- Ctrl+C – interrupts, meaning it terminates and quits a foreground process

- `%n` – assigns each process running in the background a number; by using the `%` expression a job can be referred to using its number, for instance, $ `kill %4`

- `bg` – reactivates a suspended background process

- **fg** – restores a process to the foreground

- **%? str** – used to reference the background job command containing the specified characters

- **kill** – ends a process

Batch or Automatic Processes

These processes are independent of the terminal, but they can be queued in a spooler area as they await execution on a first-in, first-out (FIFO) basis. These processes can be run by applying either of these two criteria: these tasks are executed at a specific time and date, or this is done using the at command.

The tasks can also be executed when the system load is low enough to allow extra jobs. This is done using the batch command. By default, these processes are queued and await execution when the system load is below 0.8. In larger systems, batch processing can be used when there is a lot of data that requires processing, or the task load is too demanding on the current system. It can also be used to improve system performance.

Daemons

These are continuously running server processes. They are initialized at start-up and wait in the background until they are needed. An example would be the networking daemons which lay dormant until needed by a client application. There are several Unix daemons such as `syslogd`, `sendmail`, `lpd`, `rlpdaemon`, `crond`, `syncd`, `pagedaemon`, and many more.

Process attributes

Linux processes have several characteristics that can be seen using the ps command. These include:

- The process ID or PID – a unique identification number used to reference a process

- The parent ID or PPID – the PID of the process that initiated the current process

- Nice number – indicates the friendliness of the current process to other processes. It should not be confused with process priority, which is calculated based on the nice number and the process's CPU usage.

- Terminal or TTY – indicates the terminal to which the process is linked to

• Real and effective user ID (RUID, EUID) – a process's RUID is the user ID of the owner or the user who started it. Its EUID is the user ID used to define the access the process has to system resources. They are usually the same and grant the process the same access rights as the owner, except when setuid access mode is set.

• Real and effective group owner (RGID, EGID) – the real group owner is the main group of the process owner. The effective group owner, which determines access, is usually the same, except when setgid (SGID) access mode has been applied.

The Life Cycle of a Process

A new process is created when an existing one, its parent process, makes an exact copy of itself in a procedure known as forking. This new process is referred to as the child process and shares the same environment as the parent process but with a different PID. After forking, the child process's location is overwritten with the new process data through the exec system call, hence the popular phrase fork-and-exec. A new program completely replaces the parent duplicate, even though the parent process remains with its environmental variables, standard input, output, and error assignments, along with its execution priority.

Let's use an example to help you better understand this concept. When a user runs a command such as `grep`, the user's shell process forks, creating a new process to execute the command. This new shell process execs grep begins executing the command since it overlays the shell's executable image in the memory with `grep`'s. Once the `grep` command completes, the process dies.

This is basically how all Unix processes are created. The overall process ancestor, PID 1, init, is created during the boot process. It creates other processes through fork-and-exec, and among them are processes executing the getty command. They are assigned to different serial lines and display the login prompt, waiting for someone to respond to it. When a user logs in, the getty process execs the login program, which then validates the login credentials, among other activities. Once verification is done, login execs the user's shell.

You don't always need to fork to run a new program such as is the case with the login program above. After logging into the system, the user's shell is the same process as the getty that was monitoring the unused serial line. That process switched programs two times by execing a new executable, and it will proceed to create new processes to run the commands inputted by the user. When a process exits, it sends a signal that informs the parent process that it has been completed. When a user logs out, the login shell will signal its parent, init, as it closes, informing init that it should create a new getty process for the terminal. Then init forks again and initializes getty, and the whole cycle repeats.

Controlling Processes with Different Signals

As mentioned before, processes use signals to terminate. There are, however, a lot of signals that can be used to control the behavior of a process. For instance, you can use the `kill` command to send a process a signal. Most signals are used by the system internally or by programmers when they code. Here are some examples.

- SIGTERM – signal number 15 – signals a process to terminate in an orderly way

- SIGINT – signal number 2 – interrupts a process; a process can choose to ignore this signal

- SIGKILL – signal number 9 – interrupts the process; this signal cannot be ignored

- SIGHUP – signal number 1 – this is for daemons; it instructs them to reread the configuration file

You can get the full list of signals by typing in the `kill -1` command. The list varies according to your distribution.

SUID and SGID

The setuid and setgid access modes enable regular users to carry out tasks that require privileges and access rights, which they don't have. Take, for example, in many systems, the write command belongs to the tty group. This group also owns all the terminal and pseudo-terminal files. The write command, therefore, has setgid access, which allows users to write messages to another user's terminal or window, which they normally have no access to. As the user writes, their EUID is set to that of the group that owns the executable file (`/usr/bin/write`) for the command duration.

SUID and SGID are also utilized by the printing subsystem, mailers, and other system facilities, but they are prone to causing security risks. Setuid almost always sets the user ID to root; you can see the danger this poses to the system. Programs and users can find ways to perform extra unauthorized actions, while setuid is active to retain this access after the process ends. Setuid should be avoided since it poses a greater security risk than setgid. You can perform any task with setgid in conjunction with carefully designed groups. This, however, doesn't make them completely risk-free.

System Performance Monitoring

Another important duty of a system administrator is to monitor and manage the system's performance. Linux provides tools to help with this, and these tools also give guidelines on how to diagnose and fix system performance errors. There are major resources that require monitoring and management. These include the CPU, memory, hard drive, lines of communications lines, I/O time, network time, and application programs.

Performance components are used to gauge how the system is working. Below are five major components that make up system time.

1.   User State CPU

This indicates the actual time the CPU spends running the users' applications in the user state. It includes the time spent executing user-initiated processes such as library calls but doesn't include the time spent in the kernel on behalf of the process. Every CPU time used by anything else other than the

97

kernel is marked as a user time, even if the user did not launch it. If, for instance, a user-process needs to access some hardware, it has to put a request in through the kernel, meaning this would count as system state time instead.

2.   System State CPU

This shows the amount of CPU time is taken up by the kernel. The kernel handles all low-level tasks such as memory allocation, communication between operating system processes, running device drives, managing the file system, and interacting with hardware. This means that all I/O routines require kernel services. A programmer can alter this value by blocking any I/O transfers during a session.

3.   I/O Time and Network Time

This indicates the time spent transferring data and attending to I/O requests from various processes. An iowait is a subcategory of I/O time that shows the time spent waiting for I/O operations, such as a read or write to disk. As a processor awaits a file to be opened, the time spent is marked as iowait. High iowait times can indicate issues in the system that are outside the processor's control.

4. Virtual Memory Performance

This includes time spent context switching and swapping.

5. Application Program

This is the time spent running other application programs. That is when the system is not attending to this application because another application currently has use of the CPU.

Performance Tools

Remember the tools mentioned before that help users measure, monitor, fine-tune, and manage system performance? They include:

- `nice/renice` – runs a process with modified scheduling priority

- `netstat` – prints network connections, routing tables, interface statistics, mask connections, and multicast memberships

- `time` – helps a user time a simple command or gauge resource usage

- `uptime` – shows the system load average

- `ps` – reports a snapshot of the current processes

- `vmstat` – reports statistics on virtual memory

- `gprof` – displays the user's call graph profile data

- `prof` – facilitates user process profiling

- `top` – shows all the system tasks

You can use the Manpage Help to get the syntax of these and more Linux commands.

System Logging

Linux has an extremely flexible and powerful logging system that enables a user to log or record just about anything and manipulate these records to get the information they need. This is through the syslog facility. Programs that require their data to be logged send this information to the syslog facility. syslog is a host configurable, uniform system logging facility that uses a centralized system logging process that runs the `/etc/syslogd` or `/etc/syslog` program files.

The way it works is that programs send their log entries to syslogd, which then creates the

`/etc/syslogd.conf` or `/etc/syslog` configuration file. When a match is found, it writes the log data into the wanted document. The following are some basic syslog terms you should know.

The first one is the facility. It is an identifier used to define a program or process that presented the log message. It can be the kernel, mail, FTP, etc. Next is the priority, an indicator of the log message's importance. Priority levels within syslog are defined as guides for events such as debugging or error reporting. The term "selector" refers to a combination of one or more facilities and levels. The last term is the action. This refers to what takes place when an incoming message matches a selector. They can be a write to log file, echo log message to console, send the log message to another syslog server, and so on.

Syslog facilities are programs for the selector, such as auth, which shows any activity related to requesting username and password, like getty, login, etc. Console captures messages directed to the system console. Cron shows messages from the cron system scheduler. FTP shows messages for the FTP daemon. There are quite a few facilities, and not all of them are present on all Linux distributions.

Syslog priorities show the importance of the log messages that come in. They include:

- `emerg` – for emergency conditions such as a system crash that all users are informed about

- `alert` – indicates that the message condition needs to be addressed immediately

- `crit` – shows that the message condition is critical such as a hardware error

- `err` – shows a normal error message

- `warning` – shows a warning message

- `notice` – shows that even though the condition is not an error ir should be handled specially

- `info` – for information messages

- `debug` – for debugging messages

- `none` – for pseudo-level messages that don't need logging.

These facilities and their priorities help the user discern the system logs and knows where to find the information they need. The system logger decides what to keep or discard depending on the selector priority level.

Chapter Summary

You learned what system management is and a bit of what it entails.

● A system administrator does a lot of things and thus should also be well informed. A system admin needs to know how things work, especially today, with systems being touted as easier to use and requiring little or no system administration. Simple-to-use tools are being created every day attempting to make system administration simple even for a novice.

● However, if someone has to understand the nuances and details of how things really work, it should be you.

● Before taking any actions, make sure to plan ahead.

● Remember to make the process reversible and have backups. Various tools can assist you with this.

● Implement any changes gradually and test out whatever tool you want to add thoroughly before releasing or implementing it.

Exercises

Exercise 1:

Check all the following files using the `cat` command.

- `etc/passwd`

- `/etc/shadow`

- `/etc/group`

- `/etc/gshadow`

Exercise 2:

- Connecting and disconnecting from the system

- Figure out if your system is in text or in graphical mode.

- Find the login prompt and log in with the username and password you created during installation.

- Log out and try logging in again, using a made-up username and observe your terminal.

Exercise 3

• Log in again with your username and password and change your password to K5js3.tt!, hit enter and observe what happens.

• Try it again but this time, set your password to something easy like 0000 and see what happens.

• Change your password a third time but don't input anything and see what happens.

• Try using the passwd command instead of passwd and observe what happens.

• Remember to change your password back from K5js3.tt!, after this exercise. Some systems might not allow you to recycle passwords, i.e., restore your original password within a certain time frame or a certain amount of password changes, or even both.

Chapter Five:
Security

Even though Linux has some inherent advantages over other operating systems when it comes to security, it is still vulnerable to security issues that need to be addressed just like in any other system. Regardless of the measures you may have in place, the concepts are the same. Think of it this way: the basic principles you would use to secure for your home or office will apply when it comes to computer security. You only want to let in authorized people and give them access to the areas they are allowed in. Most people think security is being risk- or danger-free. They also think that it includes the methods used to keep this danger or risk away, such as getting an alarm to keep burglars out. When it comes to computers, both these definitions apply, albeit depending on what you are referring to.

If we consider computer or system security from the point of view of being risk-free, then we are referring to such things as having reliable software, hardware, and backups. While these issues are important, this is not everything that is meant by security. Computer security also deals with preventing someone from breaking into your computer. That is, another user gaining unauthorized access to your system.

Why Is Security Important?

In today's world, almost all devices are connected to a network. Whether it is on an isolated or public network, you have to protect the system from other users and the users from each other. You don't want them altering or deleting system files accidentally or intentionally, or damaging their systems too. The odds are quite high that your Linux system will be connected to the Internet. You want to protect it from the danger that is present on the web. These intruders can impersonate a user and access a system to steal, destroy, or deny you access. This is referred to as a denial of service (DoS) attack.

An internet connection makes your system open to other systems on the Internet. While this can be great for a multitude of services, it also puts you at risk. You cannot have a truly secure system as long as it is connected to a network, but you can work to make your system more secure and robust to deter attacks.

There are many reasons why you should secure your system, and before undertaking any measure, it is important to know why you are doing so. As you look to secure your system, ask yourself what it means to be secure, what are the risks involved, the effects it will have on the users, and if there is any data on it. By considering these factors, you will know if you have met your goal of securing your system.

We keep talking about security and securing a system, but what aspects of security should be implemented to get this security? These aspects include:

- authorization for users, programs, etc. with the necessary permissions or access

- authenticity to verify users, programs, etc. as who they claim to be

- privacy to ensure personal data is not tampered with or compromised

- integrity in upholding the privacy of the data and ensuring no corruption has taken place

- non-repudiation that the data is reputable

- availability of the system to perform its duties and functions

Now that you know the aspects a secure system should have, let's look at system hardening. This chapter goes through how to harden your system to make it more secure. Before we begin, let us define some terms. They embody the key concepts of securing a system.

System Auditing

An audit is an inspection or assessment of a system. Therefore, a security audit can be defined as the inspection and assessment of a system's security capability. No system can be deemed as secure without testing. This is where a security audit comes in. You can assess the potential risks your system is under.

System Compliance

Compliance can be defined as the ability to meet specified standards. When applied to computer security, system compliance then refers to the measures taken to ensure the system meets the requirements. For instance, your baseline requires that each system should have a firewall. A compliance check would involve testing for the presence of a firewall.

System Hardening

As the name would suggest, system hardening involves strengthening your system's defenses to safeguard it better. It is similar to fortification, where you add new defenses and improve on existing ones. This fortification can also involve the removal of some components to keep the system safe. For example, if you have a security system that protects your home from thieves, you can harden it by adding other security features. These can include motion sensors, infra-red cameras, etc. to boost your defenses.

The first step is setting up a set of guidelines that explain what users on your system, even internet visitors, are allowed to do. The security level you set depends on how you use your system and the risk it is under if someone were to gain unauthorized access. A company system administrator, for instance, may want to involve the management in setting up these security policies. The system security requirements you set determine what you are securing. They identify the computer resources and data you have to protect, including the applicable laws such as privacy.

These requirements can include enabling authorized users to access data, implementing rules that define who has access to what data, and limiting access to public users. Use a robust user-authentication system tool. Refuse the execution of malicious or destructive actions on the information. Secure data from end to end as it moves across networks. Finally, impose all security and privacy needs that applicable laws require.

Risk Analysis

Risk analysis helps assess the potential dangers that could harm your system. A risk analysis defines the risk, then it identifies and establishes the priority for handling these risks. Risk analysis looks at any possible threats, what you are protecting your system against, the vulnerabilities and weaknesses in your system that could be exploited by those threats, the probability or likelihood that a threat will exploit the weakness, and the impact such a risk poses and any mitigation measures that could be taken to reduce or remove these vulnerabilities.

Threats

This is a list of typical attacks a Linux system can come under.

1.   A DoS attack

This attack ties up the computer and network so that legitimate users cannot use or access the system. Let's take a company; for instance, a DoS attack can cripple service and cause revenue losses. Since bringing an organization down with one computer attack can be hard, a common tactic is to redirect several computers to a single site and let them crash the system. This is referred to as a distributed attack, or DDoS.

2.   Unauthorized hacking

This is when an unauthorized user gains access to the system. They can steal, corrupt, or delete data.

This can have adverse effects on the system, such as causing it to crash.

3.   Disclosure of information

To disclose is to release, show, or tell something that is private. A good example would be the disclosure of a password file that shows potential hackers your login credentials. This also applies to the leakage of sensitive data such as financial or medical reports.

Vulnerabilities

Here are some of the areas in which systems and networks are vulnerable to attacks: by divulging and sharing user passwords and security credentials; through unsecured access points such as routers and network switches; the interconnections between the system and the Internet, such as gateways; loose or bad security from 3rd party network providers (ISPs); holes in the operating system's security such as internet holes associated with the `sendmail`, `named`, and `bind` commands; lastly, weaknesses in specific applications. All these vulnerabilities are potential entry points for security threats.

Securing Linux

After determining a security policy, you can

move on to securing the system as per your policy. As stated earlier, the exact steps of how you secure your system will depend on what you want to do with the system, whether it's a workstation or server, and how many users are expected to use the system. Linux security is covered in two broad categories, namely host security and network security issues, and to secure your system you have to handle both.

Important tip: if your host is connected to a large network, the directory services can present some security issues, so look into them.

Host-Security

This involves dealing with issues related to securing the OS, files, and directories. Here are some guidelines on how to address host-security problems.

1. Don't install software you don't need. For instance, if your system is a workstation, you don't need web or news servers.

2. Create all the user accounts you will need in the beginning and ensure they have strong passwords. Linux has tools you can use to enforce strong passwords.

3. Set file ownership and access to safeguard important files and directories.

4.   If your system has the capability of mandatory access control, enable it. This feature has been supported by kernels through the incorporation of Security-Enhanced Linux (SELinux) since the release of kernel 2.6. Think of it as a layer wrapped around your system, thus adding more security.

5.   Use the GNU Privacy Guard (GnuPG) to encrypt or decrypt files with sensitive data and to authenticate downloaded files. GnuPG comes with most Linux distros, and you can use the `grp` command to encrypt, decrypt and even make a digital signature.

6.   Utilize file integrity tools to monitor any changes to crucial system files and directories.

7.   Check various log files periodically for any signs of tampering, break-ins, or attempted break-ins. These files can be found in the `/var/log` directory of your system. You can install stable security updates as soon as they are made available. They target the vulnerabilities of the system and fix them. Make sure you test this update out before updating your system and machines.

8. You could spend a lot of time hardening your system and forget the physical aspect of security. What's the point of finally having a secure system if someone breaks in and steals it? You can set up your system in secure rooms where you can control access.

Using GnuPG to Encrypt and Sign Files

Linux comes equipped with the GNU Privacy Guard (GnuPG or GPG) encryption and authentication utility. It lets you create a private and public encryption key, then uses the key to encrypt your files and sends a digital authentication to show that the message came from you. Someone with your public key can verify this. The idea of using public encryption keys is basically to have two keys that are related but cannot be used to figure out one from the other. Anything encrypted with any of the keys can only be decrypted with the corresponding key. You distribute the public key to other people, but keep the private one to yourself.

Let's use an example to help illustrate the use of encryption keys. Jane wants to send a secure message to Joe. Every user generates a public and private key, and they swap their public keys. If Jane wants to send Joe a message, she encrypts the data with his public key and sends the message to him. Since the message is encrypted, it is secure from

115

eavesdropping because only Joe's key can decrypt it, and only Joe has that key. Once Joe receives the message, he used his key to decrypt the message and reads it. At this point, you might have noticed some vulnerabilities. These include, how could Joe be sure the message came from Jane? What if someone else has Joe's key and sent the message posing as Jane? This is where digital signatures come in.

Digital Signatures

The purpose of an electronic signature is to help identify you. Unlike pen-and-paper ones, digital signatures depend on the message you are sending. You first start by applying a mathematical function to the message and then reducing it to a fixed-size message digest known as a hash or fingerprint. Despite the size of your message, the digest is either 128 or 160 bits, depending on your hashing function. Next, you apply your public key by encrypting the message digest with your private key and get your digital signature. It is normally added to the end of the electronically signed message.

Digital signatures let anyone who wants to verify that you signed the message to use the public key and decrypt it to see the message digest or encrypted hash. They can run the same hash function on the message and match the computed value with the decrypted one. Since your public key was used to verify and decrypt the message, it must have been meant for you.

Using GPG

The GNU Privacy Guard (GnuPG) contains the tools you require to use public-key encryption and digital signatures. The first step is decryption, and you can get the hang of using GPG as you progress gradually. With GPG, you can generate encryption keys, exchange keys, sign files, encrypt, and decrypt documents. Let us take a look at each of these functions.

Generating Key Pairs

Type in the gpg --gen-key command. If this is your first time using GPG, it will create a .gnupg directory in your home directory, and a file named .gpg.conf will be created in that directory. It will then ask what kind of key you want. Either DSA and ElGamal (which is the default), DSA (sign only), or RSA (sign only).

After selecting a key type, hit enter. You can also hit enter to select the default choice. You will be prompted to enter a key size in bits, i.e., 128, 160, 256, etc. Press enter to accept your choice or leave it blank then hit enter to use the default value of 2048. If you want to use default settings, keep hitting enter.

117

When asked whether you really never want the keys to expire, press Y to confirm, you will then be asked to type in your name, email address, and a comment to link the key to you. Hit enter. When asked to change or confirm this data, go over it then hit enter. You will be asked for a passphrase that is used to protect your private key. The passphrase should contain both uppercase and lowercase letters, numbers, and even punctuations marks. The longer, the better, then hit enter. Be careful as you set the passphrase because you need to be able to remember it easily.

Exchanging Keys

To communicate securely, you have to give other people your public key and get their public keys. GPG stores your keys on your key ring, a file containing these keys. To list the keys on your key ring, input gpg --list-keys. To send your public key, you have to export it to a file first. The best way to document it is in the ASCII-armored format like this:

```
gpg --armor --export
spadelanny@boomee.com >
spadelanny.asc
```

This command will save the public key in ASCII-armored format in the spadelanny.asc file. The

118

key is now ready to be sent. You can also receive key files which you will import using the gpg `--import file_name` command. The gpg `-list-keys` command verify the keys present in your key ring. Next, you will want to check the key's fingerprint by using the following command: gpg `--fingerprint file_name`. This will display the messages' fingerprints. You can then verify the fingerprint and validate it. This tells the system that the key is good, and you trust the key, but be very careful with key verification as they can make your system vulnerable. You can use the gpg `-sign-key file_name` command to sign the key.

Signing Files

Signing files can be used as a way of assuring the file recipient that you have verified the information, no one has tampered with it, and you did indeed send the file. For instance, you can compress and sign a file named "urgent" using the following command: gpg `-o urgent.sig -s urgent`. Use gpg `--verify urgent.sig` to verify the signature. Sometimes you still want to sign a message to show that it came from you even though it is not secret. You can generate and include a clear-text signature with the following command: gpg `-o urgent.asc --clearsign urgent`

Encrypting and Decrypting Files

To encrypt a message, use `-encrypt` or `-e` in the GPG command, that is, `gpg -o urgent.gpg -e -r spadelanny@boomee.com message`

This message named urgent is now encrypted using spadelanny's public key. It doesn't have a signature, though. You can add it using `-s` command. To decrypt the same file, for instance, the recipient must have the private key so that they can issue this command: `gpg -o message --decrypt urgent.gpg`

Network Security

This involves dealing with issues related to threats or attacks over a network connection. Network security becomes relevant when you connect your system to a network, such as connecting to your company's internal network, even if you are dealing with a single computer connected to the Internet. Albeit the latter situation does not warrant you to worry too much, having the internal network system exposed to the world can cause you quite a headache.

You could be thinking that you can avoid putting your internal network at risk by connecting only the external servers such as the web or FTP servers to the Internet. This simplistic approach is not recommended. Liken it to an example of a person who will not drive because there is a chance they might get involved in an accident.

Not connecting your system to the Internet can have the following disadvantages. First, you cannot use file transfer protocols, or FTP, to company files from your system to the web browser. Users cannot access other remote servers that are connected to the network. The internal network users don't have access to web servers over the Internet. This makes resources such as the web inaccessible to you and your users.

A practical solution would be to use a firewall and place the webserver on a very secure host outside the firewall. You can also enable the internet services you require on your system and keep away from unconfigured services. Utilize Secure Shell for remote access and don't use the `r` commands such as `rlogin` or `rsh`. Secure and harden the internet services that you want to run on your system.

You can apply the TCP wrapper access-control files, `/etc/hosts.allow` and `/etc/hosts.deny`, to secure some of these internet services. Quickly fix any known vulnerabilities of the internet services you choose to run. You can download and install the current security updates for your distro from their online update websites.

Monitoring System Security

Even a secure system requires constant monitoring of the log files periodically for signs of intrusion. You can use an excellent detection tool such as Tripwire to detect any changes made in the system files and monitor the integrity of critical system files and directories. Your Linux system may not come equipped with detection tools; you may have to download or purchase them. Once installed, you can configure the tool to monitor any log changes.

It is essential to occasionally examine the log files in the /var/log directory and its subdirectories. Many Linux programs, such as some servers, write log data by using the logging capabilities of syslogd or rsyslogd. The log documents written by syslogd and rsyslogd are found in the /var/log directory in most Unix systems, so ensure that only the root user can read and write these files.

Securing Internet Services

For a Linux system connected to the Internet, or even one on a TCP/IP local area network (LAN) that is not connected to the Internet, a significant threat is that a user could use one of many Internet services to gain access to your system. These services, such as mail, web, and FTP, need to run a server program that responds to client requests arriving over the TCP/IP network. Some have vulnerabilities that an intruder could take advantage of to log in to your system, maybe even with root privileges. Luckily, Linux has facilities that you can help you secure your Internet services.

Switching off Stand-Alone Services

To provide internet services, such as web, email, and FTP, your Linux system has to run server programs that monitor incoming TCP/IP network requests. Some servers initiate when your system boots, and they run in the background all the time. These servers are known as stand-alone servers, and examples include web and mail servers.

Another server, xinetd, begins other servers that are meant to work under xinetd. Some systems utilize the inetd server instead of xinetd to initiate other servers. Some servers can be designed to run on a stand-alone basis or under a super server such as xinetd. The vsftpd FTP server, for instance, can be set up to run as a stand-alone server or to operate under the xinetd control.

In certain distros such as Debian and Ubuntu, you can use the `update-rc.d` command to switch off stand-alone servers, and use the `invoke-rc.d` command to commence or terminate servers interactively. To understand more about the available services, type in this command: `ls /etc/init.d`, and view all the script files meant to turn services on or off. You have to apply these filenames whenever you want to switch services on or off. To turn off the Samba service, for instance, type in `update-rc.d -f samba remove`. If the process was already operating, type `invoke-rc.d samba stop` to terminate the service. You can utilize the `invoke-rc.d command` to terminate processes or services similarly.

In Fedora and SUSE, stand-alone servers can be switched on and off by using the `systemctl` command. Input the `ls /etc/init.d` command to acquire the service scripts, then switch off a service (such as xinetd or Samba) by typing `sudo systemctl stop smb` or the proper syntax for the `xinetd` command. If the service was already operating, use `/etc/init.d/smb stop` to halt the Samba service. You can operate scripts from the `/etc/init.d` directory with the halt argument to stop any service in a related manner.

Internet Super Server Configuration

Along with stand-alone servers such as web and mail servers, the inetd and xinetd servers have to be configured individually. These servers are Internet super servers because they can launch other servers on demand. You can input `ps ax | grep inetd` to view which Internet super server, inetd or xinetd, your system operates. Debian and Ubuntu use inetd, and Fedora and SUSE use xinetd.

The inetd server is set up through the `/etc/inetd.conf` file. To disable a service, locate the appropriate line and comment it out by putting a pound sign (#) at the beginning of that line. After saving the set up file, type in `/etc/init.d/inetd restart` to restart the inetd server.

Setting up the xinetd server is a bit harder. This server reads a configuration file titled `/etc/xinetd.conf` at system initialization. This file, in turn, references configuration files saved in the `/etc/xinetd.d` directory. The files in `/etc/xinetd.d` show the xinetd command which ports to listen to and the server to launch for each port. Type in `ls /etc/xinetd.d` to view a list of the documents in the `/etc/xinetd.d` directory on your Linux system. Every file denotes a service that xinetd can launch. To switch off any of them, edit the file in a text editor, and add a `disable = yes` line in the file.

After making changes in the xinetd set up files, a restart of the xinetd server is required for the changes to take effect. To restart the server, input `/etc/init.d/xinetd restart` into the command line. This will terminate the xinetd server and then restart it. When xinetd restarts, it reads the configuration data and effects the changes.

Configuring TCP Wrapper Security

An essential security feature of inetd and xinetd is their usage of the TCP wrapper to launch various services. The TCP wrapper is a code block that provides an access-control facility for internet services by acting like a shielding package for your message. The wrapper can initiate other services, such as FTP and Telnet. However, before launching a service, it confers with the `/etc/hosts.allow` file to discern whether the host requesting the service is authorized to use that service. If nothing about that host emerges in `/etc/hosts.allow` file, the wrapper checks the `/etc/hosts.deny` file to discern whether it should deny the service. If both files are empty, the TCP wrapper can provide access to the requested service.

126

Here are the steps on how to tighten access to the services that inetd or xinetd is set up to start:

1. Use a text editor such as vi to edit the `/etc/hosts.deny` file, to include the following line: `ALL:ALL` — this setting denies all hosts access to any Internet services on your system.

2. Edit the `/etc/hosts.allow` file and include to it the hostnames that can access services on your system.

3. To permit only hosts from the 192.168.1.0 network and the localhost (IP address 127.0.0.1) to obtain the services on your system, put the following line in the `/etc/hosts.allow` file: `ALL: 192.168.1.0/255.255.255.0 127.0.0.1`

4. If you want to authorize a specific remote host access to a specific internet service, use the following order for a line in `/etc/hosts.allow`:
`server_program_name:` `hosts` — here, `server_program_name` is the title of the server program, and `hosts` is a comma-separated listing of the hosts that have access to the service. You can also enter `hosts` as a

network address or an entire domain name, such as .myplace.com.

Computer Security Tools

These are some common tools you can use as you secure your system,

1. chage – modifies the time between required password changes. You can set the minimum and the maximum number of days and the number of warning days to be given so that a change is made, and the expiration date

2. find – one of the most powerful all-rounded tools in this system. The command lets you find almost anything on a machine if you have the right syntax. Among the many choices, you can find files created by a user, by a group, or on a certain date, with certain permissions.

3. lsof – an acronym for the list open files utility. Depending on the parameters applied, you can choose to view files opened by a process or by a user.

4. netstat – lets you view the status of the network, network connections, routing tables, and statistics per interface, etc. There is

a similar command, ss, that is intended to replace much of the functionality here.

5.   nmap – scans the network and creates a map of what's available on it. This ability makes it ideal for port scanning and security auditing.

6.   passwd – allows the user to change their passwords in the command line. It shouldn't be confused with the file by the same name that has user account information. Many users don't know of its existence and opt to change passwords via the graphical interface tools.

7.   su – grants temporarily root access to another user, and can be used in the current user's session. Another shell is made; when a user exits this second shell, the user reverts to the original session. This utility can be used to become the root user or any other user as long as you have the password.

8.   sudo – instead of starting a new session (as needed in su) to carry out a job with special privileges, sudo lets the user just run that task with elevated privileges

9.   `ulimit` – sets the resource limits on shells to keep a single user from excessively hogging all the system resources

10.   `usermod` – can be viewed as an enhanced version of `chage`. It can set or change password expiration parameters and used to specify a default shell, to lock or unlock a user account, etc.

Chapter Summary

Let's recap:

•   We established what underlying security is and why it is crucial to secure your system.

•   We took a look at risk analysis and some of the threats your system might face.

•   We looked at how to protect your files and system in general by assigning users the appropriate ownership and permissions.

•   We discussed some host-security issues such as access control, and how you could use GPG to encrypt your files.

- We discussed how to handle network-related security issues and some security tools you can use.

Exercises

1.   Carry out a system security audit. Have you discovered any possible threats or vulnerabilities in your system?

2.   Check and see if your system is security compliant. Are there any ways you can reinforce your security?

3.   Download the GNU Privacy Guard (GPG) tool and install it. Try generating encryption key pairs. Were you successful?

4.   Now try to encrypt and decrypt a file. Were you successful?

Chapter Six:
Networking with Linux

Linux and networking go hand in hand. Not only is Linux the operating system of choice, but it has a wide array of tools, features and applications that allow integration into all types of network structures. Linux is preferred because of its robust nature even under heavy loads which are a result of the many years of debugging and testing.

Networking is a broad subject, and we couldn't possibly cover everything in one chapter. However, in this chapter, we will take a look at what networking in Linux entails. We will explore some of the tools and fundamental mechanisms of networking. We will also take a look at how to configure your network.

Network Protocols

The need to exchange data between machines gave rise to networking, and to be able to transfer data, computers must be able to talk to each other. However, with so many different pieces of hardware and software each speaking a different language, getting them to communicate seems complicated. How they interact is carried out in a predetermined manner referred to as a protocol. Basically, a protocol is a set of communication rules. These protocols define how each device behaves and how to react. The most common protocol in Unix-based systems is TCP/IP, which stands for Transmission Control Protocol/Internet Protocol.

TCP/IP

TCP/IP is a protocol suite containing various protocols that were developed to allow communication between different brand devices. The TCP/IP protocol suite is based on a layered model, and it is focused on delivering interconnectivity rather than adhering to functional layers. This is the reason why TCP/IP has become the default standard opposed to Open Systems Interconnection reference model (OSI).

Take, for instance, your email program. It can communicate with the OS through certain protocols but not the hardware. It would require a special program to do this and still require more software to facilitate communication between the computer and the internet hookup method used. Don't forget that the network connection hardware also needs to talk to pass along your email to the destined computer. So if all these types of communications are classified into layers, only adjacent layers can communicate with each other.

This is how the OSI model works. Even though TCP/IP is structured similarly to this, as stated before, it allows for inter-layer communication. As per the example, the network connection hardware can communicate with the email-sending application. TCP/IP protocol suite is considered the industry standard because of its versatility.

Here are some examples of the protocols in the TCP/IP family:

- Transmission Control Protocol (TCP) – a connection-oriented secure protocol. The program first sends the information to be transmitted as a data stream then converted by the OS to the correct format. The data arrives at its destination in the original data stream format in which it was originally sent. TCP ascertains that there was no data loss or any kind of mix-up. This protocol is implemented wherever the data sequence matters.

- User Datagram Protocol (UDP) – a connectionless, insecure protocol. The data to be transmitted is sent in packet form already produced by the application. The order in which the information arrives at the recipient is not assured, and there is a possibility of data loss. The UDP protocol is suitable for record-oriented applications and features a smaller latency period than TCP. For instance, Services, such as the Network File Service, or NFS, that use UDP must provide their own mechanisms to ensure packet delivery and their correct sequencing. Since it can broadcast or multicast, UDP also offers one-to-many services.

● Internet Control Message Protocol (ICMP)– this is not a protocol for the end-user, but a special control protocol that releases error reports and has control over how the machines participating in TCP/IP data transfer behave. Additionally, ICMP provides a special echo mode that can be viewed using the program ping.

● Internet Group Management Protocol (IGMP) – manages the computer's behavior when implementing IP multicast.

Most hardware protocols are packet-oriented. The data transferred to and from the hard drive is referred to in terms of data blocks known as packets. Depending on the application you are using the packet size can vary; however, they are small enough to transfer across networks quickly without any delays due to size. Also, since they are transferred so fast, you might not notice that your data is broken up.

TCP/IP Layers

If we looked at the network communication process abstractly, every section supports and is supported by the other sections. These sections, also called layers, are stacked onto each other in the order below.

	Programs/Applications	
Application	Programs/Applications	Application
Transport	TCP, UDP	Transport
Communication	IP	Communication
Security	Ethernet, ISDN, RS-232	Security
Bit transfer layer	Cable, Fiberglass	Bit transfer layer

Data Transfer

The bottom layer is responsible for the physical connection between the machines. It is known as the physical layer and deals with cable types, signal forms, codes etc. Next to it is the security layer or the data link layer. These layers handle accessing procedures such as which hosts can send data, error correction, and so on. The third layer, the network layer, handles remote data transfer and ensures that the data can be delivered and that it arrives at its destination. In more technical terms, this layer ensures that the packets either stay on the network or get transferred to the right network, all while ensuring they go to the correct network address.

The transport layer ensures that the data arrives in the right order and that no data loss occurs. It is important to note that the data link layer ensures that the data gets to the right destination while the transport layer ensures that no data loss occurs. The final layer is where the data is generated and processed by the application program. This is the layer the user sees, such as an email program.

Each layer is communicating with its counterpart on the other machine. This means that the communication between the matching layers is conceptual. The actual communication takes place between the different layers on each machine and not the matching layers on different machines. Additional data concerning each layer is added to the data packet to help each layer perform its job. This information is found in the packet header where every layer attaches a small data block, known as a protocol header, to every emerging packet.

When the application layer has information to send, it attaches the application header with the necessary information to get the data to the right destination on the receiving application. The app then calls up TCP to send the data. TCP wraps the information into a TCP packet with the TCP header added and passes it to IP. This is called encapsulation. Like the layers before, IP wraps the data packet up and adds the IP header, creating an IP datagram. The IP packet is then handed over to the hardware driver, such as Ethernet, which also adds a header and a trailer. This is called an Ethernet frame.

The network, through TCP, has a way of tracking what data belongs to what process. TCP ensures the packets are delivered in the right order and with all their content intact. It's also responsible for error detection. This is by comparing the checksum information of every data packet. If the checksum doesn't match the data packet contents or the packets fails to arrive, it is up to TCP to ensure the packet is resent. The TCP on the recipient machine must acknowledge receiving the packets; if not, the host TCP resends the packet. TCP is considered a reliable connection because of the checksum and resending data packets.

TCP/IP Version 6

IPv6, as it is more commonly referred to, is an upgrade of the IPv4 protocol. This upgrade addresses several issues regarding its predecessor such as IP address shortages, network layer security issues, IPv4's lack of mechanisms to manage time-sensitive traffic, and so on.

IP Addressing

The networking environment utilizes a diverse range of equipment to help unify them, TCP/IP determines an abstract interface through which the hardware is accessed. The interface provides a set of operations that is similar for all hardware types and basically handles the sending and receiving packets. Every peripheral networking device has a corresponding interface present in the kernel. For instance, Linux Ethernet interfaces in Linux are titled by such names as eth0 and eth1, ppp0 and ppp1 for PPP interfaces, and fddi0 and fddi1 for FDDI interfaces. These names are used for configuration purposes when you want to specify a particular physical device in a configuration command, and they have no meaning beyond this use.

Before use in TCP/IP networking, an interface must be assigned an IP address. It serves as its identification when communicating with other components. This address varies from the interface naming mentioned previously. Think of it this way: if you liken an interface to a door, the address is like the nameplate pinned on it.

The IP networking protocol recognizes addresses as 32-bit numbers, and every machine is assigned a number unique to the network environment, mainly IPv4. These addresses usually appear in the format below.

IP Address (binary): 11000000 10101000 00000000 00010100

IP Address (decimal):   192.   168.   0.   20

The IP address is written as 4 decimal numbers each 8-bits long separated by dots. For instance, a machine with an IP address of 0x954C0C04 would be written as 149.76.12.4. This format is also known as dotted decimal notation or dotted quad notation. It is increasingly going under IPv4 because IPv6 offers much more flexible addressing, as well as other modern features. The notation is split into a network number, which is found in the leading octets, and a host number found in the rest of the notation. When you apply to the NIC for an IP address, you are not assigned an address for every host you plan on using. Instead, you are assigned a network number and allowed to assign all valid IPs within this range to your hosts.

The host part depends on the network size and to accommodate the various needs several network classes showing different places to split IP addresses have been defined. Here are the class networks:

- Class A – consists of networks 1.0.0.0 through 127.0.0.0. with the network number included in the first octet section. This class has a 24-bit host part, allowing roughly 1.6 million hosts per network.

- Class B – contains networks 128.0.0.0 through 191.255.0.0 with the network number in the first two octet sections. This class provides for 16,320 nets with 65,024 hosts respectively.

- Class C – its networks range from 192.0.0.0 through 223.255.255.0, with the network number contained in the first three octet sections. This class permits for nearly 2 million networks with up to 254 hosts.

- Classes D, E, and F – IP addresses in this classes range from 224.0.0.0 through 254.0.0.0 and are either experimental or are reserved for special use and don't stipulate any network. IP Multicast, a service that allows data to be transmitted to many points on a network at one time, has been assigned addresses from within this range.

141

You may have discerned that not all possible values in the previous list were allowed for each octet in the host section. This is because octets 0 and 255 are reserved for special purposes. An address where all host part bits are 0 refers to the network and an address where all the bits are 1 is known as a broadcast address. This refers to all hosts on a certain network concurrently. So, for instance, 148.79.255.255 is not a valid host address but instead refers to all the hosts on the 148.79.0.0 network.

There other network addresses that are reserved for particular purposes such as 0.0.0.0 and 127.0.0.0. The first one is called the default route and the latter a loopback address. The loopback address is reserved for IP traffic local to your host. The address 127.0.0.1 will be given to a special interface on your host, referred to as the loopback interface, which acts as a closed circuit. Any packet from TCO or UDP will be returned as if it has arrived from another network.

Network Configuration

Most Linux distros come with various graphical tools that allow users to easily set up a computer in a local network, connect it to an ISP (Internet Service Provider) or set it up for wireless access. These tools can be launched from the menu or the command line. For instance, RedHat Linux has `redhat-config-network`, which has both a

142

graphical and a text-mode interface. Check your distribution's documentation for more information about the tools available and their use.

The tools referred to above edit particular network configuration files using several commands. The exact names and location of these files are dependent on your distro; however, there are some common network configuration files common in all systems.

/etc/hosts

The /etc/hosts file contains the localhost IP address used for interprocess communication. Do not remove this line! The file can sometimes contain addresses of additional hosts which can be contacted without using a naming service such as the Domain Name Server (DNS). You can read more about host files in the man pages, i.e., man hosts.

Here is an example of a host file:

```
# Do not remove the following line,
or various programs

# that require network functionality
will fail.

127.0.0.1        localhost.localdomain
localhost
```

```
223.168.53.10 pin.mylan.com
pin

223.168.53.11 winxp.mylan.com
winxp
```

/etc/resolve.conf

This file sets up access to a DNS server and contains your domain name and the names of servers to contact. You can get more information on the man resolve.conf page

/etc/nsswitch.conf

This file defines the order in which different name services will be contacted. The DNS needs to appear in the host's line if you plan to connect to the Internet. You can get more information on its man page.

The ip Command

This command is used to assign IP addresses to interfaces, set up routes to networks including the Internet, display TCP/IP configurations, etc. It is important to note that for two network interfaces, even on a system with only one network interface card, "lo" is the local loop, used for internal network communication; "eth0" is a common name for a real interface. Don't ever change the local loop configuration as it will lead to malfunctioning.

Wireless interfaces are normally defined as "wlan0" and modem interfaces as "ppp0", but there might be other names as well. For IP addresses, marked with "inet", the local loop always has 127.0.0.1 and the physical interface can have any other sequence. The address of your hardware interface, which might be needed as part of the authentication method to connect to a network, is labeled with "ether". The local loop contains 6 pairs of all zeros, the physical loop has 6 pairs of hexadecimal characters, of which the first 3 pairs are distribution vendor-specific.

Using netstat

This command, an alternative to ip, is used to check the host network configuration. It has a lot of options and is useful in any Unix system. You can display the routing information by using the -nr option of the netstat command.

Other commands you can use include:

• /bin/hostname – shows the name of current host.

- `/bin/ping` – sends `ICMP ECHO_REQUEST` packets to network hosts.

- `/etc/ftpaccess` – FTP access configuration file

- `/etc/ftphosts` – FTP individual host access file

- `/etc/ftpusers` – lists users who have been automatically denied FTP access

- `/etc/gated` – gateway routing daemon.

- `/etc/hosts` – lists the hosts on network.

- `/etc/hosts.equiv` – lists trusted hosts.

- `/etc/http/conf/*` – shows HTTP configuration files

- `/etc/inetd.conf` – shows the inetd configuration file.

- `/etc/named.boot` – shows the server configuration file of a named server

- `/usr/bin/rlogin` – launches the remote login program.

- `/usr/bin/route` – lets the user manually manipulate routing tables.

- `/usr/bin/rwho` – shows who is logged in on local network.

- `/usr/sbin/in.rlogind` – remote login rlogin daemon

- `/usr/sbin/in.rshd` – remote shell rsh daemon

- `/usr/sbin/in.telnetq` – the telnet Daemon

- `/usr/sbin/in.tftpd` – the trivial FTP TFTP Daemon

- `/usr/sbin/in.fingerd` – the finger daemon

- `/usr/sbin/traceroute` – traces packet routes to remote computers.

Networking Applications

Linux is a great platform for networking services and here are some of the many applications.

147

Server Types

You can provide a service to users in two ways: by letting the service run in standalone mode or make it dependent on other services for activation.

Standalone mode is mostly for those network services that are used frequently and continuously. They are independent programs that start up at system boot time, and they await requests on particular connection points or ports they are configured to listen to. When a request comes through, it is processed and the program continues listening for the next request. A good example is a web server. It should be available all the time, and if there are too many requests, it could create more listening instances to serve users simultaneously.

Program-service activation mode is for services that don't have server processes running in the background. The Internet Daemon (inetd) listens in their place and calls them up when needed, because starting all the processes you would need in a session would lead to a waste of resources and time. These services include FTP, Samba, Telenet, the secure copy or finger service, and more. The super server, Internet Daemon, is initialized at system boot and is implemented in two ways, inetd and xinetd. The latter is called the Extended Internet Daemon service, and one of the two is always running in the system.

The services the inetd daemon is responsible for are listed in its configuration file `/etc/inetd.conf` and `/etc/xinetd.conf`. When a connection request is received, the central server starts an instance of the required server. Thus when a user starts an FTP session, for instance, an FTP daemon will be running for the duration of the session. This also applies to any open connection on remote servers; either a daemon answers directly or a remote (x)inetd launches the service when required and kills it when you quit.

Other applications include email programs, web servers and browsers, FTP services, terminal emulation (Telenet), groupware applications for chatting and conferencing, news services, and so forth.

Chapter Summary

We looked at:

•   The TCP/IP network protocol and application.

•   IP addressing and how to configure your network.

•   Applications of networking in Linux.

Exercises

• Display the network information of your workstation that is the IP address, routes, name servers.

• How do you display your system's hosts file?

• What does your /etc/hosts contain?

• How can you see who connected to your system?

Chapter Seven:
Linux and Cloud Computing

Clouds can be defined as information technology environments that are abstract, pooled, and that share scalable resources across a network. They are created to enable cloud computing. Cloud computing can then be defined as the on-demand availability of these computing resources such as storage, servers, databases, analytics, networking, processing power, and more, over the Internet. Cloud computing offers flexible resources and fosters faster innovation and economies of scale. The term is used to describe data centers that are available to many users over the Internet. Here, cloud computing is an application-based software infrastructure that keeps data on remote servers that are accessed through the Internet.

Why Is Cloud Computing Critical?

The applications of cloud computing are so vast that you could be using it and not even realize it. If you use any online services to send mail, work on documents, stream media, play games, or store files, it is all thanks to cloud computing. Even though the technology is still relatively new, you can see how vast the applications are. Cloud computing is a significant shift from the traditional way everyone thought about IT resources. Here are some of the reasons why.

1.   Cost

Cloud computing has eliminated the capital expense of purchasing computer infrastructure and setting up and operating on-premise data centers. These include the endless server racks, expensive software purchases, round-the-clock electricity to power and cool these giant machines, and the IT experts required to monitor and manage the infrastructure. The math adds up quickly. With the cloud, you only pay for applications when you need them, and many are free.

The usage of these services can be adjusted to fit your needs. This pay-per-use model eliminates extra costs, such as in-house maintenance. With certain models you don't need to install software to your desktop, eliminating the need to purchase pricey software.

2.   Scalability, agility, and flexibility

Cloud computing offers more diversity, flexibility, and agility compared to other computing methods. It allows you to obtain your files from any location at any time. This can have a lot of advantages for organizations since employees can access their files from anywhere. You can also scale your usage depending on your needs. For instance, if you have a small company with only five employees, you pay for the services those five employees use. If you were to add more, you would then have to purchase more computing power depending on your needs. This would have taken quite some time in the past, but with the cloud, it is as easy as clicking a button.

3.   Speed

Many cloud computing services are provided self-service and on-demand. This means that vast amounts of computing resources can be provisioned in minutes, typically with just a few mouse clicks. This gives companies and organizations a lot of flexibility and takes pressure off capacity planning.

4.   Productivity

On-site data centers need a lot of work, from setting up the hardware, to patching the software, to configuring the servers, among other IT management chores. Cloud computing eliminates the need for these tasks. For companies, this is great because it frees IT teams to spend more time on worthwhile projects.

5.   Performance

The most important cloud computing services run on a worldwide network of secure data centers, which are regularly upgraded to the latest version of fast and efficient computing hardware. This provides several benefits over a private corporate data center, including reduced network latency for applications and more significant economies of scale.

6.   Security

Many cloud providers offer a broad set of policies, technologies, and controls that strengthen your security posture overall, helping protect your data, apps, and infrastructure from potential threats. The cloud also offers backups of all your data. It provides you with a way to safeguard your data.

7.   Reliability

Cloud computing makes data backup, disaster recovery, and business continuity more manageable and less expensive because data can be mirrored at multiple redundant sites on the cloud provider's network.

8.   Good for the environment

Cloud computing's ability to virtualize and share resources among different programs results in better server utilization. Take, for example, three distinct platforms that existed for various applications and each run on its own server. If they were to be shifted to the cloud, server resources would be shared, virtualized for the operating systems and programs to utilize the servers better. This would result in fewer servers, which would require less space, which reduces the data center size and lowers the amount of power needed to cool the servers. This, in turn, reduces the carbon and greenhouse gas emissions, thus reducing the carbon footprint. This system is not devoid of flaws, but we will take a look at those later on.

Cloud Computing Models

Cloud computing can be viewed in two ways: either as a service the cloud is offering or based on the deployment model used. Based on the deployment method used, clouds would thus be classified as public, private, hybrid, and community. Based on services offered, the classification would be as follows: Software as a Service (SaaS), Platform as a Service (PaaS), and Infrastructure as a Service (IaaS).

Public Cloud

This means that the computing infrastructure is located, owned, governed, and run by governments, academic institutions, or business organizations, and the customer has no physical control over the computing infrastructure. This cloud environment is created from resources not owned by the end-user, and they can be redistributed to other users. This type of cloud is used for business-to-consumer type interactions and excels in performance. Due to their public nature, they are prone to attacks.

Examples of public cloud service providers include Amazon Web Services, Google, Microsoft, and so on. Some of these companies also offer direct connect services that require customers to buy or lease a private connection to a peering point they offer.

Private Cloud

This cloud infrastructure is run solely for a singular person or organization. It could be managed internally or by a third party with internal or external hosting. They have the same benefits as public clouds, but they utilize private hardware. The hardware is not shared publicly, but the servers are located remotely. There are options for on-site servers, but these tend to be more expensive even though they give the user control over the physical infrastructure. This type of cloud has the highest security, although the cost reductions are minimal if the company uses on-site cloud infrastructure. Private clouds are solely dedicated to the user, and this method is used for many intra-business interactions

Hybrid Cloud

As the name implies, this cloud merges private

and public cloud infrastructure according to their purpose. For instance, a public cloud can interact with consumers while storing their data safely in a private cloud server. The public cloud is associated with scalability and flexibility in its ability to handle demand shifts. However, specific data-intensive or high-availability workloads can cause performance issues. Hybrid clouds can be used for business-to-business (B2B) and business-to-client (B2C) interactions

Community Cloud

This refers to computing resources provided for a community or organization with shared data and data management. For instance, a community cloud can belong to a government of a single company. The computing infrastructure can be located both on- and off-premises

Software as a Service

As the name implies, SaaS is the ability to access software as a service over the Internet. Application Service Providers (ASP) were a precursor to SaaS. ASPs offer subscriptions to software that is hosted or delivered via the web. The software and fees charged are based on its use. This way, the user doesn't purchase the software, but leases it as needed. You can also think of SaaS as the use of software over the web that executes remotely. The software can be in the form of services used by local programs such as web servers or remote applications accessed through a web browser. These cloud services are ideal for end-users.

Examples of remote application services include Google Apps, which provide various enterprise applications such as word processors through a standard web browser. Remote execution of applications relies on an application server to provide the services needed. A software framework that uses Application Programming Interfaces (API) for software services such as database access or transaction management is called an application server. Examples include IBM's WebSphere application server, Apache Geronimo, and more.

Platform as a Service

This service, PaaS, can be described as the virtualization of an entire platform where one or more servers have been virtualized over physical servers, operating systems, and specific programs such as Apache, MySQL, for web-based use. These platforms can be predefined and selected in some cases. However, in others, the user can provide a virtual machine image containing all the required user-specific programs. In other terms, it allows users to run applications on cloud infrastructure. The infrastructure is completely controlled by the service provider, and the user doesn't need to worry about its management or the infrastructure it is running on. The user may not know whether the underlying platform is operating on Linux, Windows, a mixture of systems, or something else entirely. All they are required to know is the interface and how to run jobs on the virtualized platform. These cloud services are ideal for software and application developers.

A good example is Google's App Engine. This service lets users deploy web applications on Google's very stable architecture. It provides users with a sandbox for their Python applications that can be referenced over the web. It provides Python APIs for data storage and maintenance using Google Query Language, in addition to supporting user authentication, image manipulation, and email sending. The sandbox restricts access to the underlying operating system. Even with limited functionality available to the user's application, the App Engine supports the building of useful Web services.

Infrastructure as a Service

IaaS is cloud computing that delivers on-demand, scalable services over the web to organizations or users who deploy workloads that can expand or shrink depending on their needs. It is the distribution of computer infrastructure as a service. This lets users run operating systems or other infrastructure over computing services. The users don't managed or have control of the underlying hardware or platforms the infrastructure is running over. They only define what service level they require and run their infrastructure over it. These cloud services are ideal for system administrators.

IaaS differs from PaaS because the virtual hardware comes without a software stack. The user then provides a virtual machine image invoked on one or several virtualized servers. This makes it the rawest form of computing as a service other than physically accessing the infrastructure. A prime example would be Amazon's Elastic Compute Cloud (EC2). In this IaaS, the user can specify a certain VM and deploy their applications or provide their VM image to be executed on other servers. The user is then simply charged for computing time, storage, and network bandwidth used.

Another example is the Elastic Utility Computing Architecture for Linking Your Programs To Useful Systems, or "Eucalyptus project" for short. It is an open-source implementation of Amazon's EC2 that's interface-compatible with the commercial service. Just like EC2, it relies on Linux using Xen to virtualize the operating system, and it was developed for cloud computing research.

Other forms of cloud computing services include security-as-a-service, data-as-a-service, test environment-as-a-service, data-storage-as-a-service, desktop-as-a-service, and API-as-a-service.

Anatomy of Cloud Computing

The cloud is a collection of services grouped in different layers, which include application, platform, infrastructure, virtualization, server, and storage. It is comprised of two major components, the front and the back end. The front end consists of the client or user part of the cloud computing system. It includes interfaces, applications, and everything needed to access the cloud computing platform. The back end, on the other hand, contains the cloud itself. It is comprised of the resources needed for cloud computing services such as virtual machines, servers, storage, and security mechanisms like traffic control and protocols. This end is under the control of the cloud computing services provider. It spreads the file system over multiple hard disks and machines. This means that the data is never stored in a singular place, and in the case a unit fails, another takes over automatically. In the distributed file system, the algorithm for resource distribution and user disk space are assigned. Since cloud computing is a distributed environment, it depends heavily upon a robust algorithm.

Virtualization and Cloud Computing

Cloud's computing ace in the hole is
virtualization; it is its main enabling technology.
Virtualization can be defined as the partitioning of a
single physical server into many logical servers. Once
the partitioning is complete, each logical server
behaves like a physical server and can perform the
same duties as a real physical server. Some of these
duties include running an operating system and other
programs independently. A lot of companies provide
virtualization services, where they let you use their
servers instead of partitioning your PC for storage and
computing. This is ideal because they are fast,
consume less time, and are cost-effective.

For software developers and testers,
virtualization allows them to write and run code in
multiple environments. It also comes quite in handy
when testing code too.

In cloud computing, virtualization is mainly
used for three reasons; network, storage, and server
virtualization.

- Network Virtualization is a way of
putting together the available resources in a
network by splitting up the available
bandwidth into channels, each of which is

162

independent of the others and can be assigned to a specific server or device in real-time.

● Storage Virtualization is the collection of physical storage from many network storage devices into what looks like a single storage device that is run from a central console. Storage virtualization is usually used in storage area networks (SAN).

● Server Virtualization masks server resources such as processors, RAM, operating system, etc., from server users. It intends to increase the resource sharing capacity and reduce the burden and complexity of computation from users.

Virtualization is the key to unlocking the cloud system, and it is vital because it separates the hardware from the software. For example, computers can use virtual memory to borrow extra memory from the hard disk. Normally the hard drive has a lot more space than memory. Virtual disks are slower than real memory, but if managed properly, the substitution works perfectly.

Cloud Security

Even though cloud computing offers great opportunities, it is not devoid of challenges. There are

163

plenty of areas at risk of being compromised and which require fortification. Below are some risk considerations that represent a potential area of attack or a source of failure. Let's examine some of the security threats and vulnerabilities the cloud comes under.

1. Organizational Security Risks

Organizational risks are defined as the risks that can impact the structure of the organization. If a cloud service provider goes out of business or gets acquired by another company, it can have adverse effects on their cloud services.

2. Physical Security Risks

The cloud data center's physical location must be secured by the service provider to prevent unauthorized on-site access to cloud service customer data. Firewalls and encryption cannot protect against the physical theft of data. It is upon the service provider to secure the data centers. They should take the appropriate measures such as controlling authorized personnel, the security of the physical location, and network firewalls. The service provider is not only responsible for storing and processing data but also sticking to privacy regulations.

3. Technological Security Risks

These are the failures caused by the hardware, technologies, and services provided by the cloud service providers. These include resource sharing isolation issues and risks linked to changing service providers - i.e., portability. Regular maintenance and audit of infrastructure by the service providers is recommended.

4.   Compliance and Audit Risks

These are related to the law, and they include lack of information jurisdiction, jurisdiction changes, illegal contract clauses, and ongoing legal cases. For instance, in some areas, cloud service providers are required by law to hand over sensitive information if the court or government demands it.

5.   Data Security Risks

There are many data security risks involved in cloud computing, but data integrity, confidentiality, and availability are the main ones. This is the area most at risk of getting compromised, and a majority of the security efforts are focused here.

At the core of all computing is the processing of raw data into meaningful information. When the processing of this data is outsourced to computing infrastructure owned and maintained by third parties, it can lead to several issues concerning the security of the data. With data security, these four properties have to be kept in check.

• Privacy – ensures that the personal information and identity of the cloud user is not revealed to unauthorized persons, especially when dealing with sensitive data. This is the most prominent problem when it comes to cloud security.

• Confidentiality – closely related to privacy. It is the service provider's guarantee that the cloud user's data will remain anonymous and safe. This can be especially hard in systems where many users have access to the same system.

• Integrity – refers to the confidence that the cloud user has that their data will not be corrupted or altered in any way by unauthorized persons as it is being retrieved.

• Availability – ensures that the cloud customer has access to their data and is not denied service due to a malicious attack on the cloud. An example of this would be a denial of service (DoS) attack.

There are three stages at which the data in the cloud can be in at any given time. The first is data-in-transit, where it is in the process of being transferred. This could mean the user is uploading data to the cloud or downloading it to their computing device. This is where data is most at risk of interception. Encryption is usually used to prevent any data loss or corruption attempts. The next stage is data-at-rest. This refers to when the data is in cloud storage. The biggest risk here would be for the user to lose control over their data. This can mean anything from data corruption to the theft of files. It is up to the service provider to ensure that they keep the user's data safe and that all four properties are kept intact. The last stage is data-in-use. This refers to when the raw data is being processed into useful information. Some of the risks here would be with data corruption during processing. Some of the ways service providers can secure their cloud computing systems are as follows.

• Service providers can employ the use of data encryption and authentication methods such as two-step authentication before granting users access to the data.

• They can ensure that cloud data centers are secured from damage and intruders. Having strong deterrents such as armed guards, or restricting access and using keycards or biometric scans, can help keep the servers and in turn the data safe.

• To prevent having malicious insiders who want to use client data unlawfully, cloud service providers should conduct an extensive background check on their employees before hiring them and also have robust measures for dealing with breaches or data leaks.

• Cloud service providers need to understand the legal and regulatory responsibilities and regulations they have and ensure that their terms of service reflect this.

Chapter Summary

We have looked at quite a lot of things in this chapter, including:

• Defining what cloud computing is, its structure, and various models

• How Linux has laid the infrastructure that made cloud computing possible

• How cloud computing is deployed as a public, private, community, or hybrid cloud

• How virtualization is the lifeblood of cloud computing and the three kinds of virtualization used in cloud computing, namely network, storage, and server virtualization

- The various security risks clouds are under, such as malicious individuals, bot attacks from malicious code that result in DoS attacks, data corruption, theft, and destruction

- Some of the ways to mitigate these risks and increase security

Exercises

1. Build a cloud Linux instance

2. Create an Amazon AWS login for yourself.

3. Go through the process of creating and connecting to an EC2 Linux instance

4. Create a key pair and download the .pem file for it

5. Now create an EC2 instance and launch it

6. Use the key file to connect to your instance

7. Try out some of the previous exercises such as running some commands to see if they work in this environment

Final Words

We have taken a long hard look at Linux in this book, and by now you know a little bit or a whole lot more about this wonderful and versatile operating system. It is the basis of significant software development in almost all industries ranging from technical areas to education. The vast applications of open-source software have given rise to countless new technologies. These include Android OS, which was developed by Google on the Linux kernel, not to mention all the distros like Ubuntu, RedHat, and Debian, to name a few. Every day more and more individuals like you are learning the benefits of using open-source software, the virus-free operating systems, and the ability to be flexible in every customization possible to suit every user's needs.

While we did not discuss the Internet of Things in this book, this is another area in which Linux is helping steer things into the future. The Internet of Things, or IoT, in summary, is the interconnection of computing devices found via the Internet that enables them to send and receive data from one another. An example is smart devices such as thermostats or air conditioning units. You can now control these and more devices using your phone. You might be wondering how all this ties into Linux. It's because the structures through which the thermostat can communicate with your phone is based on Linux and its various applications such as cloud computing.

There are several more emerging technologies that are mushrooming from open-source software such as Blockchain, which has been making big headlines with Bitcoin and other cryptocurrencies. You can see how open-source software, particularly Linux, is driving innovation. The benefits of learning Linux span further than just being able to keep up with emerging technologies. You will learn how hardware systems such as servers work since they mostly use Linux. You can even get a job or at least boost your employment chances by being Linux proficient. Its applications help companies reduce operating costs, become more reliable and resilient from attacks, and facilitate the integration of different equipment because Linux works across platforms.

The list is endless, and the vast collection of Linux distributions goes to show how limitless this system really is. There is a distro to fit any taste, and if you can't find one, build it and share it with the world. There is so much more documentation on everything you might want to know about Linux and the various distros. These include reading the man pages and the various HOWTOs available online.

This book is meant for anyone interested in Linux, whether you have no clue about it or you just want to polish up on some skills. The examples and exercises are meant to help you internalize the concepts taught in every chapter. And while it might take some time before you are called a Linux guru, reading this book is a step in the right direction.

CPSIA information can be obtained
at www.ICGtesting.com
Printed in the USA
LVHW012140010720
659414LV00016B/1168